Weird True Stories From World War 1 & 2

A Collection of Insane-But True Stories From The Two World Wars To Satisfy Your Curious Brain

(World War Trivia Volume 1)

Kimberly Miller, **History** Compacted

Copyright © 2022 by Sea Vision Publishing, LLC

All Rights Reserved.

No part of this publication may be reproduced, distributed, or transmitted in any form or by any means, including photocopying, recording, electronic or mechanical methods, without the prior written permission of the publisher, except in the case of brief quotations embodied in critical reviews and certain other non-commercial uses permitted by copyright law.

Much research, from a variety of sources, has gone into the compilation of this material. We strive to keep the information up-to-date to the best knowledge of the author and publisher; the materials contained herein is factually correct. Neither the publisher nor author will be held responsible for any inaccuracies. This publication is produced solely for informational purposes, and it is not intended to hurt or defame anyone involved.

ISBN: 9798803083924

Table of Contents

A Note From History Compacted 9

World War 1 11

Introduction 13

Chapter One A Turbulent World 21

    Franco-Prussian War 22

    Alliances 23

Chapter Two The Eastern Front 27

    Battle of Tannenberg (August 1914) 30

    Gallipoli Campaign (February 1915-January 1916) 37

    Brusilov Offensive (June-September 1916) 41

    Battle of Mărășești (July-September 1917) 45

    Battle of Megiddo (September 1918) 50

Chapter Three The Western Front 55

    Battle of Marne (September 1914) 57

    Battle of Jutland (May-June 1916) 62

    Battle of Verdun (February-December 1916) 69

    German Spring Offensive (March-July 1918) 77

Battle of Amiens (August 1918) 81

Chapter Four Heroes of WWI *84*

    Baron Manfred von Richthofen – The "Red Baron" ... 85

    Edith Cavell 89

    Aníbal Milhais 93

    Ecaterina Teodoroiu 96

    Edouard Izac 100

Chapter Five Stories & Events *104*

    The Sinking of the *Lusitania* 105

    The Christmas Truce 107

    Japan Declares War 109

    Zeppelin Raids 111

    Churchill Steps Down 115

Conclusion *117*

Trivia Questions & Answers *122*

    History Student 122

    History Buff 139

    Historian 164

World War 2 .... *193*

Introduction *195*

Chapter One Rise of The Third Reich *201*

    1935-1939: WWII Begins **210**

Chapter Two 1940: Expansion of The Axis Powers *218*

    Invasions & Occupations **219**

    Russian Expansion **227**

    Auschwitz Opens **230**

    British War Affairs **232**

Chapter Three 1941: Escalation of Hostilities *237*

    Germans Break Their Pact **238**

    Atlantic Conference **241**

    Attack on The United States **244**

    Hitler's Forces Go to Leningrad **249**

Chapter Four 1942: The Tide Turns *253*

    Wannsee Conference **254**

    Pacific Theater **256**

    North Africa Theater **263**

    Russia Under Attack! **270**

Chapter Five 1943: Alliances & Defeats *274*

    Casablanca & Tehran Conference **275**

    Russia & Germany **281**

- Allies Invade Italy 286
- Black May – Tide Turns in The Battle of The Atlantic 287

Chapter Six 1944: Beginnings of Liberation 290
- Assassination Attempt 291
- The Liberation of Paris 295
- Significant Battles of The European Theater 298
- Allies Gain Ground in The Pacific 303

Chapter Seven 1945: The Final Conflicts 308
- Concentration Camps Liberated 309
- Yalta Conference 315
- Final Battles 318
- Death of Dictators 327

Conclusion 331

Trivia Questions & Answers 337
- History Student 337
- History Buff 358
- Historian 380

Acknowledgments 401

About History Compacted 403

Dark Minds In History *405*

A Note
From History Compacted

Hi there!

This is Jason Chen, founder of History Compacted. Before you continue your journey to the past, I want to take a quick moment to explain our position on history and the purpose of our books.

To us, history is more than just facts, dates, and names. We see history as pieces of stories that led to the world we know today. Besides, it makes it much more fun seeing it that way too.

That is why History Compacted was created: to tell amazing stories of the past and hopefully inspire you to search for more. After all, history would be too big for any one book. But what each book can give you is a piece of the puzzle to help you get to that fuller picture.

Lastly, I want to acknowledge the fact that history is often told from different perspectives. Depending on the topic and your upbringing, you might agree or disagree with how we present the facts. I understand disagreements are inevitable. That is why with a team of diverse writers, we aim to tell each story from a more neutral perspective. I hope this note can help you better understand our position and goals.

Now without further ado, let your journey to the past begins!

World War 1

Fascinating First World War Stories Plus 200 Trivia Questions for Your Trivia Domination

Introduction

In 1908, Austria-Hungary annexed Bosnia-Herzegovina, a lush land to its south that had once been ruled by the Ottoman Empire. This move had been controversial both among the court of the Austro-Hungarian Empire and with the Serbian government. The Serbian government and people of this tiny Balkan nation felt that Bosnia-Herzegovina should be theirs as they had more in common with its populace.

Archduke Franz Ferdinand, the heir apparent and inspector general of the empire's army, had been one of the most vocal with his opposition. He had no love for the Serbians. In fact, Ferdinand often called them "pigs" and "thieves," among other more colorful names. However, the archduke knew that taking this land would lead to more political unrest in the volatile Balkan regions. Still, he had a job to do, and setting his opposition aside, agreed to the task sent down from his Uncle Franz Josef, the emperor. He would travel to Sarajevo in the summer of 1914 to inspect military exercises and ensure the troops were ready for combat. This decision would turn fatal and launch a series of events that ignited hostilities and a war to end all wars.

The news of the archduke's impending visit traveled quickly. Nationalism had been rising in Serbia and Bosnia-Herzegovina ever since the empire had annexed the nation. Among these nationalist and revolutionary associations was a group known as the Young Bosnians. Upon hearing of the archduke's plans, this group of radicals knew it was time to let the Austrians see the country was theirs.

So, they sat down and began plotting to assassinate the archduke. Three of the students, Gavrilo Princip, Trifko Grabež, and Nedeljko Čabrinović, would be tasked with procuring the weapons and training needed to execute the plan.

In May, these young men made their way across the Serbian border to the capital city of Belgrade. They were to meet with a group known as the Black Hand, one of Serbia's prominent liberation groups. The Black Hand was tied to the

Serbian Army, so they had access to a wide variety of weapons that would be helpful in the execution of the assassination. They delivered multiple hand bombs, pistols, and cyanide pills (to be taken if they were caught) into the hands of these Bosnian revolutionaries. For days after, the delivery shots rang out in Belgrade Park as Princip, Grabež, and Čabrinović practiced their pistol skills. When confident that they had the knowledge and skill level needed to be successful, the trio made their way back over the border with the assistance of the Black Hand.

Ignoring concerns and warnings over terrorist activity and potential danger, the archduke, accompanied by his wife, Sophie, set out from their estate on the warm summer morning of June 23. Not long into the drive, the driver and the royals began to smell something burning. They pulled to the side of the road, and jumping from the car, they found that the car axles had gotten a little hotter than was recommended and were on fire. The archduke commented, as the couple and their guards waited for the car to cool down, that this may not have been the most auspicious start to the trip. Once the minor detour was finished, the couple continued on their way, finally making it to the small resort town outside of Sarajevo that would be their home for the next week.

While Ferdinand walked lines of troops and reviewed battle strategies, Sophie took the time to tour schools and orphanages in and around the small city. Tired of the monotony of the day and the small town they were staying in, the couple made the bold move of driving into Sarajevo to stroll through the famous markets. Walking through the markets attracted some attention. Large crowds of Bosnians quickly formed, including one of the men determined to end the rule of Austria-Hungary over the nation, Gavrilo Princip.

Despite the rising hatred amongst the citizens, the crowd that gathered to watch the archduke and archduchess ramble through the markets was welcoming and polite. After this tour, the couple was scheduled to attend a banquet held by religious and political leaders, which would leave the couple with one day left in Sarajevo.

After spending the morning taking care of errands and writing to his loved ones, Archduke Ferdinand and Sophie jumped on a train bound for Sarajevo and their last day of festivities. Ferdinand would walk side by side with Sophie, an unusual occurrence for the archduchess, to conduct the last inspection of their trip before they would begin their motorcade toward the city hall. The first car carried four police officers while the royal visitors were housed in the second car, followed by a third with more security. The streets were lined with welcoming crowds, and it seemed safe enough, so Ferdinand decided it would be best to ride with their car's top down.

This would allow the couple to greet their loyal and loving subjects as they drove down the avenues. The choice to ride with their top down, however, would be a deadly mistake, for spread out amongst those adoring crowds were seven men, all members of the Young Bosnians. Security for the Austro-Hungarian conclave had been less critical than meals and political meetings, and so the archduke's route had been published ahead of the procession in order to ensure there were adoring crowds to meet them. So as the line of cars made its way down the Appel Quay, the freedom fighters took their places.

The cars passed one of the perpetrators, but the fear got the best of him, and he did not act. The vehicles moved further down the road and passed yet another, and he too lost his nerve. But as the caravan continued, the next young man and one of the three sent to Belgrade in May, Nedeljko Čabrinović, would shore his courage up and make his move. Working his way through the crowd, he arrived near the front. He watched as the motorcade approached, and leaning over to a fellow spectator, quietly asked which car was the archduke's.

The spectator, thinking nothing of the question, motioned toward the second car. As the vehicle passed by the central police station, Čabrinović pulled the pin on one of the hand bombs that the Black Hand had given him and lobbed it toward the archduke's vehicle.

Out of the corner of his eye, the driver saw something substantial being thrown at the car and accelerated. The bomb, instead of landing in the vehicle, hit the rolled-up roof and rolled backward, falling under the vehicle behind the couple. The explosion rocked the motorcade, and the crowd lined up to watch the royals as they made their way to the center of town. Several people in the crowd were injured along with two officers, but the attack had failed to affect the intended target.

Seeing that he had failed, Čabrinović pushed his way through the panicking people and jumped into the riverbed opposite the police station. While reaching for the cyanide pill in an attempt to kill himself, he was apprehended.

As he was led away in cuffs, all he would say was, "I am a Serbian hero!"

Rattled but not deterred, the archduke and his wife pressed on toward the event scheduled at the city hall. After the state event was over, the archduke and his wife demanded to visit the wounded from the earlier attack. Knowing this could be another opportunity for the dissidents to attack, the security team rushed the two into their vehicle and sped through the streets toward the hospital. As the motorcade rushed down the street, the first car turned down a small lane. Unfortunately, they had chosen the wrong road. And as the cars began to back up, the man standing in the alley, Gavrilo Princip, took the opportunity to finish the mission.

The slender young man stepped forward and drew his pistol. Two shots rang out, and the security of the royal couple sprang into action. However, it was too late. The two shots had been at close range and struck Ferdinand and Sophie. Both now lay bleeding in the cabin of their vehicle as their men tried to restrain the assailant and save their leader and his wife.

Ferdinand was hit in the neck and Sophie in the stomach. As they lay there, bleeding out, Ferdinand pled with Sophie to survive if only for their children. Alas, it was not to be as it took mere minutes before the archduke and his beloved wife lay dead.

Princip, too young for the death penalty, would admit to killing the archduke but expressed remorse about the archduchess. He would be sentenced to 20 years and die in jail before the war that he helped start would come to its conclusion.

Chapter One
A Turbulent World

World War I was a war such as the world had never seen. New technology and warfare tactics would be introduced. New alliances and rivalries would form, and the world would never be the same again. But there were already catalysts present before the first shots had even been fired.

Europe and the world had been changing, and this set the stage for the turbulent atmosphere of the time. Everything, from the final death throes of imperialism to a surge in nationalism, all contributed to the volatile state of affairs in Europe. This ever-changing world also played a role in the industrialization of war, which brought with it a wave of militarism. It seemed that Europe was a ticking time bomb.

The assassination simply was the last straw in a series of events that would finally collapse that delicate balance.

Franco-Prussian War

Many wars had been fought over the previous century, and each played a part in setting the stage for a Europe on the brink. The most recent conflict and perhaps the one that played the biggest role in prepping for the coming World War was the Franco-Prussian War. The impact that this war had on the geography of Europe would further the already-tense relationship between France and the German states. With the conclusion of the war in 1871, the newly-formed Germany would emerge a confident and robust powerhouse in the European landscape.

The Treaty of Frankfurt would eventually end the war. This agreement would cede almost all of the Alsace and a good chunk of the Lorraine to the Germans. The loss of land and the French Army's devastating defeat added to the age-old rivalry between the French and the Germans and made sure that the tension between these two peoples would live on for decades to come. In fact, over the next 40 years, those tensions would build, and when the conflict in the East began to take shape, the two bitter enemies had all the reasons in the world to take up arms against each other once again.

Alliances

Even though most of the ruling houses of Europe were related, the alliances were not formed from these relationships. Instead, it was through the imperialistic expansion during the hundreds of years leading to the 20th century and the consecutive wars previously fought that crafted the alliances. These alliances would be a critical factor in the break out of the Great War. Russia was allied to both Serbia and France while Germany was allied to Austria-Hungary. The British and the French had also signed a mutual defense agreement. The tangled web of backroom alliances and political unrest was kindling to an already smoldering fire.

In the 1880s, following the Franco-Prussian War, the Russians and Germans had developed a beneficial alliance, but with Bismarck losing grace and being removed, this relationship was lost. The new German government focused more on their relations with nations in the Mediterranean, figuring there was too much difference between Tsarist Russia and the French Republic for them to worry about the two countries teaming up. Still scathing from the defeat and land lost in the Franco-Prussian War, the French saw an opportunity, and the Franco-Russian alliance was born.

The French had ample money and a decent military to offer, and the Russians have military resources. Afraid that the new and more powerful German state would attack, the French knew they needed to build an alliance with the only other strategic force that could stand up to the Germans. After years of negotiations in 1894, the two nations signed a treaty. The agreement stated that if Germany or Italy with German assistance attacked France, the Russians would send troops. On the other hand, if Germany or Austria with German assistance attacked Russia, the French would do the same.

Another alliance that would play a part in the opening shots of the war was the Russo-Serbian alliance. Early in the 19th century, Serbians had begun to fight harder for their independence from the Ottoman Empire. The Russians still had an ax to grind with the Ottomans as they sided with France in the Napoleonic wars against Russia. So, when the political and nationalist uprising began, the Russians looked to give aid and ally themselves with the Serbs.

In the alliance of 1807, the Russians offered assistance to the Serbian rebels. Rather than live autonomously under the Ottoman rule, the Serbians took the deal. So, when Austria-Hungary declared war on Serbia after the archduke's assassination, the Russians, per the agreement, had no choice but to move to the borders to lend aid to their allies.

The entente cordiale was yet another alliance that left its mark on the world and ushered in another nation into the battle. In the early part of the 20th century, the British and French were still imperialistic powers, and this caused friction between the two nations. In order to calm the disputes in North Africa and other colonies, the two countries sat down and hammered out an agreement of mutual defense. The contract stated that Egypt would defend Britain, and Morocco would defend France. But for France, there was more involved. In fact, much like its agreement with Russia, there were safety measures in the treaty to help protect them if the ever-growing German military felt it necessary to attack France.

The last alliance that played a part at the beginning of the war was the Triple Alliance. This alliance was the mutual defense agreement between Austria-Hungary, Germany, and Italy. This treaty, like the other agreements, promised military support if the nations were attacked by France or Russia (or any of those two nations' allies).

With defense agreements in place, the battle lines were drawn, and the war would begin. On one side you would have the Central Powers (this included Germany, Bulgaria, Austria-Hungary, and the Ottoman Empire) and on the other hand the Allied Forces (this included England, France, Russia, Japan, the U.S., Romania, as well as later in the war, Italy).

Because of these alliances and ramifications of the political environment of the time, the war would be fought on two sides, dividing Europe into the western and eastern fronts and last from 1914-1918. Within these four years, over 16 million soldiers and civilians would lose their lives. This level of carnage had never been experienced, and thanks to the use of modern warfare techniques (like trench warfare) and new devastating weapons, it would become the norm in all future wars.

Chapter Two
The Eastern Front

The Austro-Hungarian Empire, shocked by the assassination of Archduke Ferdinand and his wife, knew that the aggression of the Serbian Nationalists wouldn't end there. So, the leaders of the empire gathered and decided that the only way to curb this would be to invade the small Balkan nation. But first, they would need to reach out to their friends—the Germans—and make sure that if they did that, they would hold up their end of the alliance.

Assured that Germany had their back, the Austro-Hungarian king and leaders drafted a very stern and precise ultimatum. This document was rushed to the Serbian capital in late July. There were many edicts laid out in the papers of that ultimatum, including the suppression of anti-Austrian media and the right of Austrian officials to man their own investigation into the assassination. Serbia would agree to all but one of the edicts—the independent investigation of the archduke's murder—and for the Austrians, this was enough to void the entire pact.

Feeling that this was an acknowledgment of their cooperation in the incident, the Austrians cut off all diplomatic avenues with the Serbian government and began to prepare for war. The Serbians had feared this would be the reaction, so before handing down their answer to their mighty neighbor to the north, they had sent word to their allies, the Russians, for help.

Not only did the Russians see this as an obligation, but they were also looking at the potential of gaining traction in the Balkans and the Black Sea coastal areas. So, the Russians began mobilizing their army in support of their Serbian allies. This alliance would turn this part of the conflict into a Russian/Austria-Hungary battle, just like the western front was a Franco-German war. With the battle lines drawn on July 28, 1914, just a month after the assassination of the archduke, Austria-Hungary declared war on Serbia and effectively began the Great War.

Though most associate World War I with the battles of the western front, it was the eastern front where the entire conflict began. While the world's eyes were on the newly created trench warfare of the western front and its horrors, significant battles and maneuvers were being carried out on the other side of Europe. The war on this front was not a war fought with new technology and techniques; instead, it was fought with the tried and true methods of previous wars.

For Russia, like Germany, this war would be fought on two fronts. The empire's alliance with France would force it to not only send troops to fight the Austro-Hungarians in the Balkans but also the German Army as well in East Prussia. This eastern front would be fought over a 310-mile stretch of land that ran from the Baltic Sea in the north to the Romanian border in the south. The fighting would see the Russians sending a million troops to the front to start, and throughout the four-year war, that number would jump to over three million. Though this part of the war did not see as much press in the western countries, there were still battles that would play a vital role in the length and culmination of the war.

Battle of Tannenberg (August 1914)

The eastern front began with a flurry of skirmishes that showed the vast differences between not only the equipment but also the sheer numbers of the German, Russian, and Austro-Hungarian Armies. Both Germany and Austria-Hungary, as well as their adversaries, the Russian, had greater distances to move than those fighting on the western front, and this led the Germans to decide to leave just one army cohort to protect the East Prussian border. The distances would also play a part in keeping this theater of the Great War more traditional in its tactics and movements. In the end, Tannenberg would be a devastating loss for the Russians. Through logistical and strategic miscalculations, the Russian Army would be crushed in just over a week.

With their French allies in the west feeling the pressure of the onslaught of German military movements, the Russian commander-in-chief, Grand Duke Nicholas, answered their call and began preparations for a significant military move against the Germans. The grand duke, feeling that the sheer number of Russian troops would be enough to pull German forces from the western battles, deployed his first and second armies to East Prussia. However, though they were many, the units were not fully prepared to engage in the intense battles ahead. The grand duke had signed off on the plan to mobilize his troops into action too early, but the fault for the ultimate defeat at Tannenberg fell squarely on General Yakov Zhilinsky.

Zhilinsky had held the position of chief of the general staff for several years and would keep his job during the first few months of the war until the mistakes and miscalculations of the Battle of Tannenberg would come to light. When the war broke out, France called on their Russian allies to help with the fight, and Zhilinsky answered that call with a promise to mobilize 800,000 men within the first two weeks of the war.

The Russian forces were not ready for this expenditure of men and equipment, and so there was a lot of pressure on not only the troops but also the military leadership. This promise would cause the Russian leadership to make some very rash decisions. Overextending and over-promising were the biggest of those. Not only had Zhilinsky promised an excessive amount of men, but he had also promised the French that he would attack both the Germans and the Austro-Hungarians simultaneously, and this stretched his resources very thin. For the Prussian campaign of his military mobilization, Zhilinsky chose to use two of his armies, the

First Army led by General Rennenkampf and the Second Army led by General Samsonov.

The plan was simple. The First Army would move into East Prussia from the east, which Zhilinsky felt would cause the German Army to move defensive forces from the French line to shore up the woefully inadequate troop count stationed there. Then two days later, the Second Army would move up from the south and attack the German forces from the rear, cutting access off to Vistula River (in what is today's Poland), which would give the Russians control over a significant transport lane. The plan on paper was a solid one and one that caused the Germans to spring to action quickly once the news of the impending attack was relayed to command.

However, where this strategic plan failed was in the execution. On top of poor leadership and the Russian Army's lack of readiness, two logistical miscalculations led to the utter devastation of the Second Russian Army.

The first of the logistical oversights was the distance and geography that separated the two armies. In between the two armies were the Masurian Lakes. The lakes stretched over 50 miles, and that, coupled with Königsberg, a highly fortified area, would hinder a rapid advancement from the south by Samsonov's men. This geography would narrow the route to just 40 miles and would limit Rennenkampf's ability to advance as fast as they would need to meet Samsonov's army from the south. Unfortunately for the Russians, the Germans knew this and would use it to their advantage in the coming battle. The second issue was one that was more of a problem for Samsonov's troops. In preparation to paralyze the German forces and keep them from invading Russian territory, the military divisions before them had desolated the railways and destroyed roads, which though was intended to hinder the German advancement, made it difficult for their own troop movements as well.

On August 17, Rennenkampf's First Army would begin their push into East Prussia. The troops moved in a flurry against Germany's Eighth Army commanded by General Max von Prittwitz. The battle was furious, but eventually, the larger Russian forces, despite their inadequate training, were able to push back multiple German divisions of infantry and cavalry. The first battle waged on for three days, and by the time that it had come to a decisive conclusion, Samsonov's Second Army was able to get into position for the next phase of the battle. However, due to the hurried pace, Samsonov's men were tired and hungry; not all the supplies had been able to make it, nor had the entire cohort, which left them at a disadvantage.

Unfortunately for Samsonov, his troop's movement and their location were spotted. On August 20, Prittwitz received word that the Russian Second Army was approaching from the rear and that the numbers were significantly more than the army to the north. These revelations seemed to worry General Prittwitz, the man in charge of the Eighth Army, and so he sought council with several of his most regarded subordinates.

In this meeting, he expressed concern that the Russian force moving from the south would cut off any route of escape and put forth a plan to take his troops and set up behind the Vistula River. Despite the strong opposition to this plan from both General Grünert and Lieutenant Colonel Hoffman, the general still felt his way was the best. Though eventually, he would be convinced that his strategy was too risky and move on to another option.

An offensive would be launched on Samsonov's western flank. In preparation for this maneuver, Prittwitz moved three divisions from the north and integrated them with the soldiers of the XX Corps. Then the general would have the rest of the northern troops retreat to the west. With the troop movements, the Eighth Army's headquarters moved to Mülhausen. The maneuvers executed, Prittwitz soon received word that his men had been able to break away from the advancement of Rennenkampf's forces and that the tactics had stalled the movement of Samsonov's troops. But that wouldn't be the only piece of news relayed to the general. His inaction and insistence on retreating to Vistula to hold the line there had alarmed the German leadership back in Berlin. Realizing that the eastern front of the battle was going to be just as tricky as the western front, they had decided to replace Prittwitz with proven leadership. A train was on its way, and on it was the division's new leader, General Paul von Hindenburg (future President of Germany), and his chief of staff, Erich Ludendorff.

Ludendorff and Lieutenant Colonel Hoffman (one of Prittwitz's former advisors) corresponded back and forth and would join together to create a plan. They would form this plan using Hoffman's experience and knowledge of the Russian Army, which he had gained while observing the Japanese during the Russo-Japanese War. The plan would decimate Samsonov's troops. The tacticians would attack Samsonov's left flank again this time with the power of six different divisions. The first step was to send for reinforcements from the north as the number of soldiers currently available to the Germans was less than the Russians of the Second Army.

Calling for these reinforcements was a gamble, as it left just a cavalry front to hold the defensive line against Rennenkampf, who was still advancing near Gumbinnen. The reinforcements would sweep up from Samsonov's right while the already-present troops would advance on his left. The two German forces would push through, surrounding the center of the Russian cohort and blocking Samsonov from moving on his target.

These were risky maneuvers as they entailed large troop movements to go unnoticed by the enemy. However, the lack of communication between the two Russian generals and the German's ability to decipher the wireless orders sent by Samsonov to his troops made the German troop movements very easy to keep hidden.

After several tactical victories over Samsonov's flanks, the Second Army's core was cut off from any means of escape. The Russian troops became a hungry mass of untrained soldiers, and despite efforts to push through, they realized that the end was near. To protect his troops and himself, Samsonov ordered the remainder of his forces to turn south. Knowing that the roads would be watched and patrolled by the German forces, he urged his troops into the woods, and without knowledge of the area and with very little hope, his cohort would end up lost in the dense forests.

The general, painfully aware that all was lost, strolled, unbeknownst to his advisors, into the woods on the morning of August 30. Amid the frustration and fear in the camp, a shot rang out. The general had taken his own life instead of dealing with the shame and potential capture by the German forces. And with that one bullet, the Battle of Tannenberg came to an end.

Gallipoli Campaign (February 1915-January 1916)

The Dardanelles Campaign, also known as the Gallipoli Campaign, was a British and French operation in Turkey. After the Russian leaders appealed to their allies—the French—and, in turn, the British, for help, the two Allied Forces banded together and set out for the Aegean Sea. The two forces hoped they could occupy Constantinople and gain control of the straits that joined the Black Sea with the Aegean. The occupation of the straits and Constantinople would cut off the Ottoman Empire from the Caucuses and ease the stress on the Russian forces. A victory would be a pivotal part of removing the Ottoman Empire from the war altogether, thereby weakening the Germans and Austro-Hungarians' position and leading to the end of the conflict. Unfortunately, the campaign would be riddled with miscalculations and underestimations.

Between 1904 and 1911, the British had toyed with the idea of moving on the Ottoman Empire to gain further control in the Middle East. Once the idea was examined closer, it was deemed likely to be a devastating defeat and was put on the back burner. Yet, when war broke out in 1914 and the Turkish allied themselves with the Austro-Hungarian Empire, the British and their allies—the French, felt it was worth retaking a look at this proposal. So, when Grand Duke Nicholas asked for help in January of 1915, the British took the opportunity not only to settle their interests in the region but also to help their Russian allies by cutting off the Turkish insurgence into the Caucasus front. When the British decided to help the grand duke, they knew that the Dardanelles was the place to execute this maneuver. They also knew that it would take a massive collaboration between both the main military forces and the British naval fleet.

Led by then First Lord of the Admiralty, Winston Churchill, the British command decided to run a solely naval driven operation at first. Not wanting to use their best ships as they were needed in the North Sea to hold the barricade there, the British decided to use warships that were too old to be in commission. The use of old ships would protect their endeavors in the North Sea, and if the campaign failed, there would be minimal loss of money and useful ships. However, that plan was short-lived as it soon became very evident that there would also have to be ground attacks. The shores of the Dardanelles would have to be taken and held so that the fleet could do its job. So, with this decision firmly in play, a British military presence began building in Egypt along with a small contingent from their French allies to aid their seafaring brothers in arms.

On February 19, the initial battle was set to begin, but the weather would not permit it, and so the operation was halted. After six days of inclement weather, the skies cleared, and the mission could move forward. Marines landed, accompanied by combat engineers set for demolition duties on the beaches without any opposition. Still, the weather turned quickly, and this portion of the mission would stall just like the initial launch. It wasn't until March 18 that the actual barrage of bombs began in preparation for the fleet to make their move. After several hours of bombardment, the British had lost three ships, and several more were damaged. The loss of these ships was a clear sign; this mission was going to need more than the might of the fleet.

After regrouping and restructuring their plan, the mission continued in late April. This time, troop transports amassed on the island of Lemnos with the intention of landing in two pivotal places along the Gallipoli peninsula. On April 25, the British forces would land at Cape Helles, and the ANZAC (Australian and New Zealand forces) would take the other beachhead. As the battle progressed, the Allied armies moved forward, securing small beachheads along the way. However, these victories were small and difficult to obtain as the insurgents were met with Turkish resistance, led by the man who would later be known as Atatürk, Mustafa Kemal.

The British forces struggled to gain land and needed to find a strategic tipping point for their next landings. Three months later, on August 6, another wave of soldiers landed at Suvla Bay. The Turkish had moved troops from this location as they felt the British would never attack it (though one commander, Mustafa Kemal, warned that this would be the location but was dismissed) because it was a naturally fortified region. So, the Turkish leadership had left a bare-bones presence. Even with the limited troop resources, the Turkish forces were able to stop the invading forces in their tracks eventually, thanks to their knowledge of the landscape and the natural fortification of the bay. With all the unsuccessful pushes and attempts to take the Dardanelles, the British felt it was time to replace their leader, and in September, would do just that. However, it was too little too late.

By late November, it was evident that the campaign would not be a victory for the British and French forces, and in waves, the Allied Forces left the shores of Turkey. By the first week of January 1916, all troops had been evacuated. The British's bid to take the straits and help the Russians had failed, and dealt the British a devastating defeat.

Brusilov Offensive (June-September 1916)

In February of 1916, the Battle of Verdun began on the western front. In response to this, the French called on their allies to help them out. By having the British and the Russians attack different fronts, the French hoped that a chunk of the German forces would move to shore up the holes that these offensives would open up. This tactic had worked in previous instances, so why not try it again? Both the British and the Russians agreed. This agreement would lead to several battles, including the Battle of Somme on the western front and the Battle of Vilna and the Brusilov Offensive on the eastern front.

The Russians initially attacked at Lake Narocz in Belarus. That campaign did not end well for the Russian Army. The Russians would begin this conflict with a barrage of artillery attacks. Unfortunately for them, they were inaccurate and would do little damage to the German artillery. The Russian troops, once the artillery had finished, would cross No Man's Land between the two armies in groups instead of spreading out. This miscalculation would make these troops easy targets for the still intact German artillery. The poor artillery execution would lead to a demoralizing defeat for the Russians and require them to regroup and try again. So, with that defeat, the Russian military began to plan a diversionary tactic near Vilna, which is now part of Poland. This battle was a disaster as well, and the Russians desperately needed a battle that would hold up their end of the bargain.

While these attacks were being executed and done so poorly, there was a Russian force sitting in the southwest part of the eastern front. This force was commanded by the highly experienced general named Alexei Brusilov. He and his troops sat, with no plans from the big brass coming down for them to do anything other than holding the line and keep the Austro-Hungarian forces from moving into Ukraine.

The elderly general knew him, and his extremely well-prepared troops could be of more use, so he sent word to the Russian military leaders asking if he could have permission to make a move. His troops were recovered from their previous victories, he had plenty of supplies, and he believed his men could handle the campaign. Many of the generals back in the capitol felt that this maneuver would end up being the same disaster as the others had been, but Brusilov pushed them harder, knowing he could be successful.

The brass finally agreed but didn't expect very much from this offensive, but they would be proven very wrong. Brusilov took the time to train his troops using full-sized replicas of the intended targets. This training allowed his men to calculate with precision where to aim their artillery. He used air reconnaissance to gain knowledge of these locations' layouts and defenses and kept this all under tight wraps until his troops were ready to execute the offensive. Starting the assault on June 4, in the city of Lutsk, Brusilov and his troops laid siege to the Austro-Hungarian Fourth Army lead by the Prince of the Habsburg Dynasty, Archduke Joseph Ferdinand. Shocked at the precision and brutality of the Russian attack, the Austrian line was demolished on the first day of the offensive.

Over the next two days, Brusilov led his men through Lutsk, devastated the Austrian troops, and gained 50 miles of territory. Once the Austrian forces were on the brink, the units of Slavic soldiers deserted them, leaving them to the mercy of the Russian troops. The first battle was successful, and Brusilov would push on in the hopes of making even more gains for his beloved Russia. This well-executed push led to over 130,000 casualties and the capture of 200,000 prisoners. The Battle of Lutsk was just the beginning of his march, and over the next several months, he continued to devastate the southwestern line of the eastern front.

The offensive would be carried out along about a 200-mile stretch of the front that started from the Pripet Marshes down to the Carpathian Mountains of Romania. With nearly 2,000 guns, Brusilov's men pushed forward even though the numbers favored the Austro-Hungarian forces. However, with the rapid-fire onslaught, the Russian troops overwhelmed the Austrian line, perhaps because the Austrian forces underestimated the Russians' preparedness. Once the Austrians were pushed back to the Carpathians, they realized that they had underestimated the Russian forces and had lost too many supplies and men, so they reached out to their allies for reinforcements.

Eventually, in September, the push had exhausted Brusilov's supplies, and with no further help coming, the offensive had to come to an end. But by the time the offensive had ended, Brusilov and his men had captured approximately 400,000 men and 10,000 square miles of land. The push had tarnished the Habsburg's reputation as well as the military career of the prince. Along with that, two other military campaigns had felt the repercussions of this unexpected attack. Austrian military forces had to pull back from efforts to take the Trentino region of Italy, and the western front had several German divisions rerouted to help reinforce their allies, which, in the end, may have cost the Germans the Battle of Verdun.

Battle of Mărășești (July-September 1917)

The Romanians had entered the war in 1916, and immediately became a focus of the eastern front. One of the last and main battles of the Romanian campaign was the

Battle of Mărășești. By the spring of 1917, the eastern front and the Russian military had been driven into chaos and disarray. With issues at home, the Russians had become unfocused, and the Allied Forces on the eastern front had experienced a series of devastating losses. In the hopes of turning the tides back in their favor on the Romanian front, the Russians (what was left of them) and the Romanian forces began to make plans for a two-pronged plan that would push the Austrians out of Romanian territory permanently. The first attack would be on the area surrounding Nămoloasa, and then once the damage had been done there, the combined forces would attack the Germans and Austrian troops in and near Mărășești.

However, before they could launch the first attack, it was abandoned, and the troops meant for that battle were relocated to be support for the Battle of Mărășești. The forces of the two adversaries were pretty evenly matched; however, the Romanians, being strategic, had shored up sections along the attack route with extra troops, which would benefit them strategically in the long run and swing the needle in their direction. The attack then started with two days of heavy artillery on the German and Austrian positions aided by well-scouted aerial reconnaissance.

The ground offensive would begin with the Romanian Second Army flanked by the Russian Ninth and Seventh Armies going up against the Austro-Hungarian First Army. Still, with the two days of intense bombardment, this force had been shocked and was a little unsure of what was happening. Phase one of the battle would lead to Romanians taking the Teiuş hill in the village of Mărăşeşti. In the early morning of July 24, the two divisions would flank the forces and clear the path, eventually leading to them holding the Încărcătoarea clearing.

The second phase would start simultaneously with the previous maneuvering and the Fourth Romanian Army Corps pushing left across the land toward the Coada Văii - Babei clearing. At the same time, in the southern portion of the battlefield, the Romanian Second Army would be moving toward the same clearing, then the front line would begin moving to the hills north of Lepşa. Here, the Romanians felt they had an advantage over their enemies as they were used to fighting in this rugged and uneven terrain.

The German and Austrian forces were warned about these plans but felt that they could easily defend themselves and eventually land their own counter-attack that would halt the Romanian Armies' march. Unfortunately, the

Romanians' familiarity with the land and love for their homeland would dash the German/Austrian forces' hopes.

The Austro-Hungarians and Germans planned to rely on their defensive lines and preparations to halt the Romanian advancement. These defenses came in two different forms, which had been used to much success in other parts of the war. The first was structures they called resistance centers. These were a series of trenches that were connected and covered by artillery. At crucial junctures, these trench systems would be topped with a steel dome and other military implementations to help form a shelter. In these junctures, troops or munitions would be stored, and these enclosures were intended to help keep them safe as well as give the troops housed in them a tactical advantage.

The other aspect of their defensive line was trenches. Hurriedly crafted over the last few weeks, the trenches that had been dug were remarkably well-crafted. Though the trenches were executed masterfully, the two defensive techniques could not match up to the knowledge and drive of the Romanian Armies. The Romanians quickly figured this out and used their air force to do reconnaissance to find these points and would concentrate their attacks on them with excellent results. The Romanian Army, coupled with the efforts of the air force and the people of the villages surrounding the battle, used the rough terrain to their advantage and carried out short and swift attacks on some of those weaker positions. Before they would make any moves though, the Romanian Army would volley a major artillery attack on the German and Austrian troops before beginning their ground and air assaults.

In August, the Romanian Army would lose support from the Russians, as the hostilities back in Russia continued to escalate and the revolution required them to return home. After a decisive counter-attack led by August von Mackensen, the Romanians and the Austrians would continue to battle back and forth, neither gaining any significant ground. This back and forth would continue until both side's reinforcements were depleted, and they had to give up and consider the Romanian Campaign a stalemate.

Eventually, over the next few weeks, Romanian cities and states would continue to fall as well as the lands that surround the nation. Eventually, this would lead to the signing of the Treaty of Brest-Litovsk, where the proud Romanian leaders and military would end up surrounded by Central Powers. In turn, this would lead to the Treaty of

Bucharest in 1918, where they ceded lands to Bulgaria and bartered for peace with the German forces.

Battle of Megiddo (September 1918)

In August of 1915, the Ottoman Empire quietly joined the Central Powers and the war. In alliance with the Austro-Hungarian Empire and the newly formed German state, they hoped to be able to carve a little land out for themselves in both the Caucuses and the Balkan states. The Ottomans also wanted to regain power over the areas that once were part of the empire. Countries like Egypt and the Balkan states were among these lands. By the time the armistice was signed on October 25, both sides had lost vast numbers of soldiers, but the battle would still go down as one of the most decisive victories fought in Ottoman territory.

The first significant attack of the Ottoman campaign would be in January of 1915 on the Suez Canal. With a victory in the Sinai Peninsula, the forces, then led by General Murray, felt emboldened and pressed further into Ottoman territory in the hopes of taking Palestine. Once the British troops pushed through the Suez and into Sinai, the next two battles for Gaza came up short. These losses would be bad news for the commander of these battles because, with these losses, the powers back home decided they needed a new person leading the campaign. General Sir Edmund Allenby was the man they chose. This change of command would be significant and directly lead to the Battle of Megiddo.

Allenby brought with him a great deal of wartime experience as he had fought in the Boer War as well as the Battle of Ypres and many more. In particular, the general was well-versed with cavalry maneuvers and leading them to success. This experience gave him an advantage when it came to mobilized campaigns. He also didn't play by the rule book when it came to strategies, and that may have been the reason that the campaign was so swift and decisive. The plan he laid out to his superiors was one of these out of the box ideas. He looked to surround Gaza and gain control over Beersheba by taking the long way around. Allenby planned to drive deep into the desert and encircle Gaza. This maneuver would be the best way to spring a surprise attack on the Ottoman forces.

Though this maneuver seemed like one that was doomed to fail by many of his peers, it was just the thing that the British needed to break through and open up the possibility of taking Jerusalem. By the time the summer rolled around and the hard rode trail had been completed, it was easy for the Australian Light Horse brigades to ride in and take Beersheba. This victory opened the Gaza Strip up and left the road to Jerusalem free for the taking. Maneuvers like this had put the Ottomans on the defense. The British forces had managed to push the Ottoman forces out of Palestine, and this left them attempting to regroup and course-correct at Megiddo.

The Ottoman Army, now regrouping on the plains of Megiddo, may have thought that they were safe, but Allenby had already devised a strategic plan of attack that would take them by surprise. He wanted to trap the Ottomans on the plains and not give them any way to escape, and that was precisely what he and his troops did. The attack would be a simultaneous and coordinated attack using everything, from infantry to the cavalry, to tanks as well as planes.

The battle would start at Sharon. A group of Arab rebels, who were part of his troops, would focus on breaking the Ottoman lines of communication. At the same time, divisions of Indian and British soldiers would overrun the Ottoman forces. The battle would start with a very precise artillery bombardment, and once that was done, the infantry would push in and breach the Ottoman's defenses. After that, the Desert Mounted Cavalry (DMC) would be the third wave of attack. The Battle of Sharon was quick, and by the time night had begun to fall, many of the Ottoman strongholds and cities had fallen. That left the way open for the next essential part of Allenby's plan: an attack in the Judean Hills.

The Battle of Nablus would start with the infantry breaking through the Ottoman defenses in the hills. Along with the Chaytor's Force, a division of Allenby's troops that were comprised of both cavalry and infantry, the forces would work to take the Jordan River. At the same time, the artillery helped reduce the Ottoman Eighth Army's defenses. While all this was going on, the Ottoman Fourth would be attacked as well. The multiple pronged attacks would have battles lasting through the night. At the same time, the DMC completed their task of encircling the Ottoman troops, and this left the Ottomans open for the next phase of Allenby's plans.

Once the Ottomans had nowhere to go, all that was left was to cut off supply chains, and that meant using that new military weapon, the plane. British forces, along with their Australian compatriots, bombarded the Wadi el Fara road, the main supply chain of the Ottomans, until the Ottoman troops and divisions were defenseless.

These maneuvers allowed for the remaining British forces to easily take the Ottoman soldiers as prisoners and conquer any fortifications that were left.

Chapter Three
The Western Front

Though the fuse was lit with the archduke and his wife's assassination in mid-July of 1914, the war on the western front would not officially begin until August 3 (a week after the war started on the eastern front). The Russians' support for the Serbians had forced their hands on the eastern front, and militarization had begun. With its alliance to Austria, Germany soon declared war on Russia, but knew by doing this, they would be drawn into conflict with Russian's allies, the French. This act would give the Prussian military and the new German state the chance to enact a strategy that they had been holding in their back pocket, the Schlieffen Plan. Crafted by Alfred von Schlieffen (the former chief of staff of the German Army), this plan laid out a distinctive course of action for a two-front war that the Germans would bank on for their total victory.

On August 3, the plan came to fruition as German troops moved to the border of their neighbor and neutral nation, Belgium. Before this militarization, the German leadership had sent King Albert, the sovereign ruler of Belgium, a strongly worded suggestion that he let them pass through his territory on their march toward France. This brash tactic got the attention of the British, as Belgium had been deemed neutral. This neutrality had been in place since the signing of the Treaty of London in 1839. In response to Germany's ultimatum to the Belgian ruler, the British also sent a warning to the German governing body in Berlin to stop their plans of invasion or feel the wrath of the British military. London gave them a full day to reply, and when they had heard nothing by the deadline, the British declared war.

Neither of the sides thought the war would take long. The Kaiser even told his troops in his send-off speech that they would be home by the first week of August. There were some generals on both sides that knew different, but even with that knowledge, they did not strategically prepare for a long war. Not preparing the people or troops for this inevitability would be the biggest mistake known to man, as the war would rage on for four long years and cost millions of lives.

Battle of Marne (September 1914)

The German forces advanced across Belgium and into northeastern France, looking to capture Paris. That hope shattered with the German force's decisive and bloody defeat at the First Battle of Marne. In September of 1914, the German troops seemed to have a clear path to Paris and felt as if their conquering of this critical city was a forgone conclusion. But that celebration wouldn't be in the cards. The mass marching and insurgent attacks by divisions of the French Army would help put a tactical victory on the scoreboard for the French and their newly arrived allies, the British Expeditionary Forces (BEF).

After a month of marching through Belgium, the German Army finally crossed the Marne River and entered French territory early in September of 1914. This brazen strategy ignited fear within the French people and the government. So, to protect their assets, the French leadership made a bold move. They knew that if they stayed in Paris, the Germans would capture and torture them endlessly. The French did the only thing they could and moved their leadership south to the city of Bordeaux. Even with news of this tactical withdrawal, the Germans still felt Paris was the objective. It was the heart and cultural center of the country, and by capturing it, the Germans knew they would break the French's fighting spirit. Once that was done, the Germans would then be free to turn this attention to a much greater enemy, Russia.

The conflict waged on, victories ebbing and flowing between the two mighty empires. This initial battle of WWI could have gone either way, but thanks to some tactical miscalculations and a little luck on the French leadership part, the fight would go down as a win for the Allied Forces. The tactical miscalculation would be carried out by the leader of the First German Army, General Alexander von Kluck. But even before he could make that critical error, the French had stumbled upon a fortuitous piece of intelligence.

As the French and British forces were pulling back to regroup from one of the many small conflicts, an Allied soldier came on a fallen German infantryman. Like with any other battlefield, the Allied soldier bent down to check if the other man was still alive. Once the soldier realized that this German was dead, he began to look for supplies that he could use and found a backpack. His hands fumbled to get the bag open, but when he did, he began to rifle through it. Pulling a piece of paper out, he saw that scribbled in German across it was the battle plan that the soldier and his entire regiment were ordered to carry out.

The soldier folded the paper up and quickly found his commander to pass on the intel that he had so haphazardly found. The commander looked at the plan and realized that the French had been planning for the wrong attack. Until that moment, the French military leaders were sure that the German's First Army would march through the Oise Valley. Instead, the plan laid out in front of them showed that the Germans planned a more direct approach. The First Army would march and attack Paris head on! The leader of the French Army, Joseph Joffre, moved quickly and began to reinforce and move troops to defend their capital from the impending attack.

Using air reconnaissance and radio intercepts, which had never been done before, the French Sixth Army, led by Michel-Joseph Maunoury, moved into place, and waited. General von Kluck, getting word of the French troop movements, hurried his troops to the north to meet the advancing French forces instead of sticking with the original plan of marching on Paris straight on. This tactical choice would open the German front line up to some sound countermoves by the alliance of France and Britain. Making this decision would lead to three bloody and challenging days where the tide would continually turn along a hundred-mile stretch of land.

On September 6, General Michel-Joseph Maunoury and his Sixth Army Division, who had been standing their ground much to the chagrin of the German military leadership, received reinforcements. The close proximity to Paris had allowed for the use of public transport and taxis to help with the war effort. Over 5,000 troops arrived fresh and ready to protect their beloved Paris. Along with the soldiers, enough supplies to keep the French and British forces stocked for a little while longer also arrived. These transportation methods would become the first use of motorized transport and gained the moniker "Taxis of Marne." The preparedness of the French Army caught von Kluck by surprise, and in a matter of hours, he had moved his advanced guard back to the main body of the army. The now recombined forces raced to cut off Maunoury's troops. Unfortunately, this would lead to the German general losing contact with the Second Army lead by General Karl von Bulow, stationed on his left flank, and created a substantial breach between the two forces.

The breach created by this division of the German forces filled in with the troops of both the French Fifth Army and the BEF splitting the German forces in half. The inability of the two forces to communicate left the two German generals at a severe disadvantage when it came to outmaneuvering the Allied Forces. As the French Army began to pivot into the German's right-wing, many of the German divisions attempted with all their might to close the breach and stop Joffre's attacks. The efforts of the soldiers though were in vain, and General Bulow, just three days later, would order a retreat, understanding that this battle was lost and that there were more secure locations that his men could attack from and defend. Two days later, General von Kluck would come to the same conclusion and pull his troops back as well.

The two armies would pull back to the lower Aisne just 40 miles east from the present battlefield. The French would pursue them to the Aisne, and unfortunately, here they would lose leverage and end up in a stalemate. To prevent the Germans from losing any more ground, the German leaders would instruct their men to begin digging ditches, and so the trench warfare was born. Trying to outmaneuver and outflank each other, both forces would continue this practice and create a defensive standoff. This constant trench building would become known as the "Race to the Sea" and would leave the French and Belgian countryside with miles and miles of barb-wired topped trenches for the next four years.

The German Army overextended both their logistical information and their firepower. Though led by a brilliant tactician, Helmuth von Moltke, the battlefield decision of his leaders left the German Army unable to reach their goal of taking control of France by invading its capital, Paris. The installation of miles and miles of trenches by the German Army was a direct response to the Schlieffen Plan's defeat and would also serve as a signal to the Allied troops that this conflict was not going to end quickly. These trenches would see some of the most inhumane circumstances and leave a whole generation scarred from diseases and psychological trauma.

Battle of Jutland (May-June 1916)

The Great War would be fought mostly on land, but the seas were not barren of epic conflicts and decisive victories. In the Spring of 1916, one of the largest and most famous battles was fought on the waters of the North Sea. The Battle of Jutland was to become the most massive naval confrontation in all of history and would hold this title until the next Great War and the Pacific Theater. The conflict would be a battle that was a tactical win for the Allies, but at such a high cost, it would be hard-pressed to call it a total victory. With 151 ships, the British Grand Fleet would square up with the German's much smaller fleet of 91 boats. The strategic goal of this maneuver was to continue blocking Germany's access to the open waters of the Atlantic. In that respect, the Battle of Jutland was an unmitigated success.

The Battle of Jutland's story starts at the very beginning of the war in 1914, in the halls of the British special intelligence agency known as Room 40. As the war began, the codes used to relay military maneuvers and troop movements were still very simple. Most relied on old-world cavalry and sailor signals that were easy to decipher and known to just about anyone. For the German military complex, the use of wireless telegraphs to send messages was new. This fact led to them not giving much attention to the code publications provided to their soldiers.

There were three publications, and luckily for the Allied troops, a copy of all three of the German codebooks was obtained very early in the war. In fact, most of the German codes were cracked before the first battles of the war even began. So, from the beginning, the British forces, both land and sea, were able to listen to every instruction relayed to the enemy troops and make tactical decisions based on them. The cracking of these codes would allow the British fleet to intercept the plans of the German Navy and help them plan accordingly.

Then in 1916, Reinhard Scheer replaced Hugo von Pohl as the chief of the High Seas Fleet, of what is now the world's second-largest naval fleet only being surpassed by their enemies, the British Grand Fleet. This change in leadership brought with it a shift in strategy (one that would eventually serve to bring the Americans into the war in 1917). Vice Admiral Scheer knew that though the German fleet was mighty, it had nothing on the British Navy's experience and size. For this reason, he moved to a lure, trap, and destroy strategy. Using this strategy would allow the German fleet to gradually dwindle the might and forces of the Royal Fleet, making the German's strategic standing better for a massive scale attack at a later date.

This strategic command translated to the directive to attack British merchant vessels. Specifically, those merchant ships that had routes that took them along the coast of Norway. It also meant planning for a logistical move to take out one of the British fleet's battlecruiser squadrons commanded by Admiral David Beatty. After deploying U-boats to key vantage points, the German High Seas Fleet set out to the north to set up on the coast of Norway. This squadron sailed with several battlecruisers as well as light cruisers commanded by Vice Admiral Franz von Hipper. At a reasonable distance behind Hipper's ships, Scheer would, with the remainder of the fleet, follow and pin Beatty between the two forces. Unfortunately, thanks to the cracking of the German naval code by the codebreakers of Room 40, Admiral John Jellicoe, the commander of the British fleet, was fully aware of the German admiral's plans and began his own countermeasures. Jellicoe intended to catch his adversary off guard and to execute a much larger scale naval maneuver.

The sun was high in the sky when the light cruisers under von Hipper's command spotted the ships of Beatty's squadron. Ready to take his adversary on, Admiral Hipper turned to face them. At 3:22 in the afternoon on May 31, the first salvos of the Battle of Jutland sailed through the air. Though ahead of schedule, this encounter seemed fortuitous to Hipper, and he looked to win his glory by drawing Beatty's ships closer to the main body of the approaching German fleet. In the first hour of the conflict, the Germans seemed to have the upper hand as they were able to sink the

British vessel, the *Indefatigable*, and damage several other ships.

In response to that, Beatty moved his battlecruisers to the front. The heavy guns of the British battlecruisers lambasted the German ships, and soon Hipper's squadron was in trouble; it seemed the tides had turned. Moving to block the barrages of artillery, Hipper commanded his destroyers forward to shield the rest of the ships. As the German destroyers formed their line, they also released a flurry of torpedoes, and, in doing so, were able to sink another British battlecruiser. During the initial conflict, both sides took a considerable amount of loss and damage.

As the battle waged on, a message came through to Beatty. A British patrol squadron had spotted a large mass of German vessels heading in his direction. The plan was clear now: the German Navy was trying to sandwich Beatty between the two forces in the hopes of devastating it and weakening the position of the entire fleet. Knowing he had to react quickly, Beatty turned his ships and headed northward, where he knew Admiral Jellicoe waited. Beatty knew that not only would this help reinforce his already damaged forces but also draw the split German fleet toward a more extensive, more dominant one.

Beatty arrived at the location of Jellicoe's squadron, and both forces sat peering to the south, waiting for the Germans to be visible. Finally, 45 minutes later, at 6:15 in the evening, with the sun beginning to set, the location of the German fleet was spotted. The admiral, wanting to end this battle, swiftly radioed for his ships to form a battle line. He did not want to fight in the low light of dusk, which would heighten the danger of the conflict. With his ships anchored end to end, Jellicoe knew that the German ships would only be able to use their forward guns effectively. This strategy was a maneuver known as "Crossing the T." This fact would give the British a significant advantage when it came to firepower. As the Germans approached closer, Jellicoe and his fleet unleashed a barrage of fire, forcing Scheer to turn his vessels 180 degrees in an attempt to gain some distance between the two navies. Using a smoke screen laid out by his destroyers, Scheer scurried away in retreat. This smokescreen, coupled with the last rays of the sun, made visibility bad, and Jellicoe was left wondering what had happened.

However, the maneuvering of the British fleet had, in essence, used the very same tactic that Scheer had planned to use, and the German fleet ran smack into the rest of the British fleet just an hour later. Scheer, attempting to make the same tactical retreat as before, wound up, leaving his fleet in a worse position. Within 30 minutes of the renewed conflict, the Germans were feeling the effects of being outmaneuvered. To save the bulk of his fleet, Scheer made a Hail Mary order and deployed his torpedo boats to run headlong into the British Navy. Though this would mean losing some ships, it was a gamble that paid off as Scheer was able to turn his fleet and begin his long voyage back to his home port. Even with this tactical retreat, the two fleets would continue to have small clashes throughout the night. As the sun rose on June 1, Scheer and what remained of his fleet had been able to limp back to Wilhelmshaven, and the mighty naval battle had come to an end.

Both sides claimed victory, and in truth, both sides were victorious in their own right. The Germans sustained fewer injuries and loss of vessels. On the other hand, the British had lost somewhere in the realm of 6,100 men and several ships that would equate out to about 113 tons of metal. The Germans had only lost about 2,500 men and 62,300 tons. When it comes to achieving their ultimate goal, however, the British were the winners. They were able to maintain their blockade on the Germans, and that meant keeping the German fleet from having access to the open seas and more merchant routes.

Battle of Verdun (February-December 1916)

The Battle of Verdun would end up being one of the most bloody and lengthy offensives in the war. It would see troops moving into enemy trenches as the lines moved forward and backward, having to live in squalid surroundings with heaps of decomposing bodies. The battlefield would end up with dead soldiers beaten to bloody messes from heavy barrages of artillery strewn across miles of the French countryside. These fields would be home to some of the most horrific atrocities of the war. This campaign would be a war of attrition. By the time the 11-month battle was over, there would be over 700,000 casualties. This carnage was the result of the mindset and tactics of a prominent German military mind, General Erich von Falkenhayn.

General Erich von Falkenhayn would send word to the Kaiser himself and lay out how he thought the Germans could win the western front. The general argued that Britain was definitely formidable but that taking Britain would only be possible with the use of U-boats, and that would be difficult with the British strength when it came to their navy. Instead, mercilessly attacking the French and inflicting so much torment and damage on their ally, France, would be the only way to get Britain to the peace table and win the war on that front. So, taking France was the key to either a German victory or defeat. There would be no stealthy maneuvers and could be no peace treaties. Instead, the only way this war would be won, Falkenhayn believed, was to inflict as much damage as possible, both when it came to property and human lives.

Thus, attrition would be the name of the game if Germany hoped to take France. This notion was not a well-received one. However, the Kaiser eventually approved the campaign, despite his and the other leaders' misgivings. The defeat of this crucial part of the Allied Forces would not come with mass troop movements into their territory, rather a strategic choice of location and then the constant barrage of attacks that would bleed France into submission. They would need to choose the right site for the battle first. The chosen site had to be a place that could break not only the French Army's spirit but also its power as well. The best option would be a symbolic location that the French would give their lives to protect and one that would benefit the future movements of German soldiers into the French countryside. After studying the maps, Falkenhayn settled on Verdun.

Not only was Verdun a tactical gem, but it was also a precious sight for the French people and a significant location for the Germans as well. For the Germans, the town held a special place in their hearts as it was the site of the signing of the Treaty of Verdun in 843 A.D. The signing of this treaty would split the Carolingian Empire up. This separation would help create the states that later became the core of what was the new German nation. The ancient city was also one of the last occupied by the Germans in the Franco-Prussian War. After the loss and formation of a new German border, the French built the city into a heavily fortified stronghold to protect it from future German aggression. The Verdun fortress along the Meuse was threatening German communications as well, which needed to be taken care of immediately. By occupying this citadel, the German forces would be killing two birds with the same stone—taking a strategic point on the front line and dealing a death blow to the French. Or at least that is what Falkenhayn thought.

To maximize the efficiency of the general's plan and the landscape, the Germans would have to attack with several rapid burst advancements. This tactic would serve to pull the French reserves to the front and directly into the extensive artillery line put in place by the Germans. To start these advancements, rapid and intense artillery barrages would be executed. This tactic would allow the Germans troops to move quickly and shore up the land gain before the French could bring more reserves to the front or plan a counter-attack. Once the plan was finalized, it was then laid out for the operations commander, Prince Wilhelm, the oldest son of the Prussian ruler. The Prince had little military experience and was swayed by the passion and conviction of Falkenhayn. The first stage would be to shore up their forces in the vicinity of Verdun, and doing so without being seen would be difficult.

Over several weeks, Falkenhayn and the commanders of the army began moving artillery and troops forward using the hilly landscape and air cover to keep their movements secret. But first, they would need transportation and shelter, and this was done by building a railway line as well as concrete bunkers at the destination site. With these in place, Falkenhayn and Prince Wilhelm began moving their supplies and armaments. The Germans, over several weeks, were able to move several tons of artillery and munitions, not to mention thousands of troops and all under the not so watchful eyes of the French forces stationed in the region.

It wasn't until early January that French reconnaissance planes noticed that there had been some ramping up of German troops, but at the time, the French didn't seem to be too concerned. Then in early February, the news of the size of the German build-up on the banks of Meuse was relayed properly to French intelligence. With this new intel conveyed to the leaders of the French Army, they began to improve the defensive capability of the Verdun region hastily. To slow this process down, the German forces started to cut off access to the central railways. The French quickly course-corrected. Instead of using the railways, they began to use the "Marne Taxi" idea and developed routes for a motorized supply chain. This 37-mile road (which would become known as the La Voie Sacrée) would be a crucial part of the French defenses for the entirety of this brutal conflict. It took over a week for the French to get supplies to their front line because of the German machinations. But in that time, large quantities of weapons and men were moved to the front, and the French felt they were ready for whatever the Germans would bring, but they were wrong.

With both armies in place, in the early hours of February 21, the Germans began to execute their plan. With 25 miles of front line armed with massive artillery, they began to bombard the French. When the initial hail of artillery finished, the Germans sent out scouts to investigate the damage. If the French defense were devastated, German scouts would signal for a push of the infantry, and if the defenses hadn't been crushed, the message would be sent to begin the artillery bombardment once again. In the late afternoon, the defense was finally ripe for the picking, and the German infantry began to push forward, followed by combat engineers and then the main body of the German forces. This process would repeat multiple times until the field was covered with piles of corpses and the enemy driven back. Over the next few days, the German military gained quite a bit of leverage breaking through the first line of the French defenses. The troops and supplies had been depleted. Both sides took some time and rushed to bolster their positions as well as forces.

Though the French during the initial German push were able to save one city, the rest of the French defenses were wiped out rather quickly. The significant loss to the Germans caused the higher-ups in the French government and military to reconsider the leadership at the front. They would replace the "Victor of Marne," General Joffre, with General Pétain. This change of command also came with a fresh and ready-to-fight army. The task for these new troops was to hold the right bank no matter what. Though initially, the powers-at-be wanted to amass the French forces on the left bank to stop the Germans from crossing, the higher ground of the right bank was thought to be easier to defend.

Four days after the first battle, the Germans neared Fort Douaumont, which was one of the fortifications built up after the Franco-Prussian War. The French, busy with their troop movements, never saw the attack coming. The Germans quietly approached the bastion and found a passageway that was left unguarded. The small squadron worked their way into the catacombs under the city and was able to, without spilling any blood, round up the 57 French soldiers left to man the fortress. This victory was bloodless and would be celebrated by Germans near and far. The Germans would hold this fort for eight months before the French were able to regain the stronghold. Eventually, the retaking of Fort Douaumont would be one of the victories that would turn the tides of the battle. Taking this tactical position back was followed by the French chasing the German Air Force out of the skies over Verdun. The Germans would mount a counter-attack, but even after that, the French held firm at Douaumont.

In June, the Germans would receive the news that the eastern front had taken a huge hit. Russian General Brusilov (see Chapter 2: The Eastern Front - Brusilov Offensive) had just unleashed a devastating defeat to the Austro-Hungarian forces. Moving these troops would mean that many of the resources destined for the Battle of Verdun were diverted to the front line in Ukraine. The final French Summer Offensive was unleashed on June 24 and commenced with an artillery bombardment that lasted a full week. Then the infantry pushed in after this. The Germans were able to repel it but took heavy casualties (as did the Allies). The back and forth advance and retreat continued for the next few months, but in September, the tides would turn in favor of the French and their allies. Then came the news that the British were converging on Somme, and with this two-pronged attack spurred on by the pleading of the French generals, the death knell had begun to ring for the Battle of Verdun (though it would take another four months to end ultimately).

Eventually, in mid-September, one of the French generals that had helped maintain the line of the right bank proposed a strategy that would deliver Verdun back into the hands of the Allies. General Charles Mangin suggested using similar tactics as his German counterparts had used to gain their foothold. The movement would start with a massive artillery bombardment followed by an infantry insurgence. With the reduced forces due to both the Battle of Somme and the Brusilov Offensive, it wasn't long before the French had taken back several of the cities that had fallen into German hands over the last several months.

The general, who was okay with the loss of his men, would attempt the same tactic in early December. However, the weather would postpone that maneuver. This little hiccup allowed the Germans to learn of the plan and launch their own counter-attack. This preemption wouldn't last long, and soon both sides were under furious fire from their enemies. On December 18, the French would reclaim Chambrettes and capture thousands of German soldiers to end the battle that had raged on for almost a year.

German Spring Offensive (March-July 1918)

As the war began to wear down, the troops on both sides felt the fatigue and psychological effects of fighting for almost four straight years. Knowing this, the leaders of the German military attempted one last push. The goal of the Spring Offensive was to deliver a definitive blow to the allies and reinvigorate the German military force. The plan for the offensive began in late 1917, when General Erich von Ludendorff, the First Quartermaster General, began to consider a reinvigorated offensive strategy.

With the looming inclusion of America's massive army and the collapse of the war efforts on the eastern front due to the victorious Russian Revolution, Germany was able to reallocate resources. Because of these factors, it made sense to plan an offensive. There would only be one shot, though, as the attack is needed to be executed before the U.S. could replenish their troops. With the decision finalized and approved by Ludendorff's commanders, the general began to plan this offensive.

The German tactician selected a 50-mile stretch of the front line that was defended by the British Army. Attacking the British Army instead of the French was a calculated tactic and one that, if the general had set a territorial objective, may have just worked. The British military was less war-experienced than the French or the Germans, and this led the Germans to look at them as easy pickings.

The miscalculation of not defining territorial objectives allowed the general to miss out on some strategic points that could have turned the tides of not only this conflict but also the war in general. Vital weak points like the vulnerability of the British at the rail hubs of Hazebrouck and Amiens could have been substantial targets if he had focused his troop's efforts on them. This concentration on the weak points would have allowed Ludendorff the ability to cut the British off from supplies and reinforcements.

Instead of focusing on these strategic points, Ludendorff went into the mission with two distinct goals. The general wanted to push his way in between the French and British Armies. Once this had been accomplished, with the less-experienced British Army separated from the French, the general planned to move north and annihilate the British line. Lastly, he planned to use psychological warfare and tactical advantages to Germany's benefit. Once separated from the French, who were familiar with more combat tactics than trench warfare, Ludendorff felt the British would be easy to defeat and quick to surrender.

Once Operation Michael's plan (the Germans' codename for the first phase of the Spring Offensive) was finalized, all that was left was to choose the time. On March 21, 1918, in the early morning hours, the Germans moved onto that 50-mile stretch of the Allies' line chosen by Ludendorff as the objective. The British forces had been alerted to the attack but were unprepared for the newly-reinforced German military and the might of their artillery. With heavy barrages of artillery and blazes of bullets, the Germans launched their attack, aided by the dense fog that blanketed the land that morning. For five hours, this constant bombardment went on, and once the general felt that the line was significantly weakened, the infantry and cavalry moved through the line.

The initial result was excellent, with the German military advancing over quite a distance thanks to their month-long training to prepare for the offensive. When the initial push of the assault was complete, the Germans had taken a good amount of land and almost 100,000 prisoners. This "victory" was not one at all though, as Ludendorff had made one significant error. After this advancement, he assumed the British Army had been defeated and moved several units to the south to stop the French from sending reinforcements. This decision split his force and left his attacks less impactful, which would hurt the campaign significantly in the long run. Though the first phase of the offensive technically was a success due to the land gained, none of the lands that had been acquired held any tactical or strategic value.

After the initial push, the Germans would repeat this tactic down the 50-mile stretch of the front line. Each of the subsequent offensives (codenames Operation Georgette and Blücher) were failures for Ludendorff and his troops. Whether it was from tactical errors, like splitting his army up, or being tricked into launching a full attack when he didn't have the resources, the rest of the Spring Offensive would see defeat after defeat for Ludendorff and the German Army. On July 18, the French moved on the weakened German forces in a surprise attack, and from then on, the war was in complete control of the Allies, and the Spring Offensive had been crushed.

Battle of Amiens (August 1918)

The Battle of Amiens would be one of the final battles of the war and was the first of the Allied offensive that would come to be called the "Hundred Days" campaign. The Battle of Amiens was a direct result of the ineffectiveness of the German Spring Offensive. With the failure of Ludendorff's Spring Offensive, the Allied Forces looked to execute their own campaign. The inability to capture Amiens as a critical tactical point due to the railway hub by Ludendorff left General von der Marwitz in a little bit of bind. That, coupled with the unsuccessful last German offensive at the Second Battle of Marne, left the German Army open for an Allied push. The Allied invasion would aim at securing and retaking strategic hubs such as Amiens, which would allow them to move supplies and troops more effectively. The Allied Forces would be reinforced with troops from several nations, including the U.S.

General Ferdinand Foch understood the need for an offensive with this objective and looked for the first acquisition to be the securing of the railway hub at Amiens, which was a vital line to Paris. In August, along with his allies, Foch began consistent and rapid attacks on the German line. These attacks would leave the Germans little to no time to recover and would be the deciding factor in the war. While these attacks went on, troops had deployed to bolster the forces of the Fourth Army commanded by General Sir Henry Rawlinson that would move on Marwitz when ready.

When it was all said and done, one of his units included 14 infantry divisions made up of soldiers of Australia, Britain, Canada, and the U.S. He also had control over tank units and cavalry as well. These nightly exercises would give him the element of surprise and be one of the things that gave the Allied Forces such an advantage over their German adversaries at the Battle of Amiens.

Armed with many tanks and guns, the forces were supported with aircraft from both the British and French. This massive army was to face Marwitz's Second Army, which was comprised of ten divisions with limited supplies and equipment. Coupled with the demoralization of the German Army after the Spring Offensive, the stage was set for an Allied victory. On August 8, in the early morning hours under cover of fog, the British began their attack. Over the next few hours, the advancement of the Allied troops would show their might and destroy the first German defensive line. In a later memoir, Ludendorff would call August 8 as the "Black Day." This battle gave the Allies territory, but the demoralization of the German troops is what Ludendorff refers to with this moniker.

Other parts of the offensive did not fare as well, but on the whole, the Battle of Amiens was a success. By August 12, the Allies seemed to have gained all they could, and Field Marshall Haig called the battle done and moved to prepare an offensive to the north. The fighting would continue for several more months, but shortly after this Allied victory, many German higher-ups, including the Kaiser himself, had already accepted their defeat.

Chapter Four
Heroes of WWI

When it comes to defining what makes a hero, it can be tough. Is it the soldier who follows his orders even when he doesn't agree with them? Or the soldier who goes against the rules to ensure his men get home safe? Is it the nurse that risks her life to save innocents from the terrors of war? Or is it the pilot who heroically takes down multiple enemies, protecting his people and furthering his country's cause?

The truth is, these situations can all be called heroism, and WWI has some fantastic stories when it comes to bravery and those who put their life in the line of danger for others and their country. These stories below are of people that come from many different backgrounds and fought on both sides. Still, one thing is for sure, for whatever side they fought on, they were heroes that showed courage and conviction in the face of unknown terror.

Baron Manfred von Richthofen – The "Red Baron"

Known to the world as the "Red Baron," Manfred von Richthofen was born into a well-respected Prussian military family. He would also become one of the biggest heroes of the German people during WWI. Living by the motto "Go for the lead pilot first" between 1916 and 1918, the flying ace would gain notoriety by shooting down 80 Allied aircraft. The Allied pilots that flew through the skies over the battlefields feared looking out at the horizon and seeing the Baron's patented red plane, knowing that this may very well be the end for them. His precision and ruthlessness would end up making him a propaganda machine for the Germans and turn him into a national hero.

Born into a noble Prussian family in the Spring of 1892, it was a foregone conclusion that he would find himself standing in the Prussian military complex. Spending his youth hunting and playing sports, young Baron Richthofen would appease his stern and proud Prussian father by enrolling in military school at the very young age of 11.

Here, he would continue to excel, and by the time he was 17, he would have his first commission.

Working his way through the grades, he would graduate in 1911 and was assigned to a cavalry regiment. When the war broke out, his unit saw action on both the front line of the western and eastern fronts. It was there that he began to make a name for himself. With bravery and dedication, he and his cavalry unit would travel along the front lines, and for his courage, he earned an Iron Cross.

The war quickly turned, and eventually, his cavalry unit was assigned the mission of maintaining and distributing supplies up and down the trenches of the western front. The repetitive, tedious assignment felt to Richthofen a little too menial for a Prussian of his standing. So, he appealed to the higher-ups to transfer him to the German Air Service. The German command, because of his reputation, approved this, and Richthofen would find himself as a backseat observer in the reconnaissance planes of the German Air Service.

Sent to do reconnaissance on the eastern front, Richthofen would take the summer of 1915 to earn his pilot license in between his reconnaissance missions. The transition between the backseat and the front seat was challenging (he even crashed on his first solo flight), but Richthofen pushed through the process. Once he had his license, he began taking combat missions over France and Russia. During these missions, he met the famed pilot, Oswald Boelcke, who saw potential and recruited him into the newly formed fighter squadron, Jasta 2.

It wasn't long until he had absorbed everything that he could from the seasoned fighter pilot and began building the reputation he would become known for, including gaining the title of flying ace after his first confirmed aerial victory in September of 1916. Richthofen would rack up quite a tally over the coming month, having 16 confirmed victories, putting him squarely on the top of the leaderboard. The German ace was so proud of his work that he felt he needed to commemorate his triumphs. So Richthofen sent word back to a Berlin craftsman and started having silver cups created for each of his aerial victories. He would amass 60 of these before the silver shortage would put an end to this practice.

Because of his fearless work on behalf of the German military, he earned the highest honor a military man could receive, the "Blue Max," and command of his fighting squadron, the Jasta 11. It was at this time he decided he needed to make a change and painted his plane that iconic red that the pilot would be known for, and that would birth the moniker he would go down in history with, the "Red Baron."

The "Red Baron" would have a stellar season in the spring if 1917. He would take down another 36 enemy planes to bring his total up to 52. It was clear he was approaching legendary status, and the German leadership began to realize he was the perfect propaganda tool. Hence, they started handing him every military decoration they could and put his face on newspapers, magazines, and even postcards. Soon the "Red Baron," a symbol of German excellence and pride, was whom every little German boy wanted to be, and every German girl wanted to marry.

After a productive spring for him and his squadron, Richthofen got another promotion and took charge of his very own fighter wing, Jagdgeschwader 1, otherwise known as the "Flying Circus." Taking a cue from their leader, the squadron decided to paint their aircraft with bright colors, and the pilots chosen for this division were, like the Baron, able to fly effortlessly through the air, much like a trapeze artist did through the air of the big top. It would be at this time that the Baron began flying the red triplane that would be his most famous aircraft.

The legend would come to an end in April of 1918. Engaging a squadron of British planes flying over the Somme Valley in France, he and his squad would battle bravely through the air. As Richthofen swooped down low to follow his target, Australian machine gunfire sprayed from the ground, surprising the pilot. The ground fire, combined with the fire from the Canadian pilot Arthur Roy Brown, would have the German flying ace on the run. During the barrage of gunfire, Richthofen would take a bullet straight to his upper body and plunge headfirst to the field below.

Crashed behind enemy lines, the German flying ace's body was recovered by the Allies and given a respectful and proper burial that would suit his heroic status. The legend was dead, and for the Allied pilots, the skies would be a little safer.

Edith Cavell

The hero nurse of Belgium, Edith Cavell, fought to keep soldiers alive to the very end. Standing up for what she believed, this soft-spoken nurse would save over 200 men's lives and help them get safely out of occupied Belgium. But she did not discriminate; she fearlessly lived by the motto, "I must have no hatred or bitterness towards anyone." This dedication to saving lives came later in life but would be the attribute that wrote her name in the annals of history and tragically would bring about the end of her life.

Edith was born in 1865 and spent the first quarter of her life walking the streets of Swardeston in Norfolk, England. She worked as a nanny, but this was not fulfilling nor what she wanted to do for the rest of her life. She was a caring young lady but wanted to find a path of her own. Then tragedy would befall her father, and being the oldest child, Edith took on the duty of nursing him through his severe illness. As she diligently oversaw his recovery, she soon realized that she had finally found her calling: nursing.

Edith, now sure that medicine was her future, began to find places and classes to learn everything she needed to be a successful nurse. She worked in several hospitals throughout London and soon became well-known amongst them. A visiting surgeon from Brussels worked alongside her and saw the potential and the care Edith gave her patients. He urged her to join him back in Brussels, and with some serious convincing, she decided that it was an excellent opportunity.

In 1907, Edith moved from her native country to Belgium. It wasn't long before she had built up a reputation.

The surgeon who had convinced her to uproot her life also suggested that Edith begin training nurses as her bedside manner was just what every ailing individual would need and want. So, she took his advice here as well and began to teach her skills and methods to other young women. Eventually, it led to the founding of the Berkendael Institute, Belgium's first nursing school.

In 1914 however, things were going to change drastically. Belgium was in the direct line of the German Army's plans to take France. As the German troops advanced through Belgium, they also occupied it, feeling as it would give them a strategic advantage over both the French and the British. With an occupied Belgium, they could have a clear path for reinforcements and a strategic post to watch their enemy movements closely.

Edith Cavell, a citizen of one of these adversaries, would seem like a dangerous person to leave amidst your newly conquered lands. But with the school becoming a Red Cross hospital, the Germans had no recourse (at the time) to remove her. Though they had no way of relieving Edith of her post, the Germans did not trust her (or any of the nurse and staff of the hospital), so the Germans, using spies and informants, would continually monitor movement within the institute's walls. So, Edith's school was allowed to remain open and would begin treating soldiers from both sides.

Edith Cavell could have abandoned her post, but she knew that she was needed, so she stayed. Eventually, she would join the Belgian Underground and begin rescuing Allied soldiers stuck behind enemy lines. Cavell used her institute to house these soldiers and used her ingenuity and wits to throw the Germans off their trail. Along with her compatriots, she created an underground path that led to Holland and then back to England, which allowed many men to find their way back home and to safety.

Cavell rescued hundreds of soldiers before the German spies that watched her discovered her betrayal and began to make preparations to end her extracurricular activities. In August of 1915, the Germans had accrued enough information to accuse Cavell of what they felt was a horrible betrayal of their trust. She was arrested and charged with treason. Taken to St. Gilles Prison in Brussels, she would await her trial.

Nearly a month later, her trial would finally begin. During her hearing, she was asked a handful of questions, and with confidence and dignity, answered honestly.

Question after question was asked of her, and each she answered with full voice. Then, she was asked how many soldiers she spirited away to safety. She straightened her back and spoke clearly, "I have saved hundreds of lives and would not hesitate to do so again!" This question would be one of the last items asked of her. Deliberation was quick, and sentencing was even quicker. Edith Cavell had been found guilty of treason and was sentenced to death by firing squad.

On October 12, Edith Cavell and other conspirators were taken out to a courtyard, and in a hail of bullets, their lives would come to a tragic end. When word of this execution became known to the world, it caused outrage, and for her bravery, she has been remembered ever since.

Aníbal Milhais

When most people think of the combatants of WWI, they think of Germany, Austria, France, England, and even the U.S., but many other countries sent troops to the front line. One of those was Portugal, which had abstained from the war for the first two years. However, the neutral nation had no choice but to enter once Germany surprisingly declared war on them in 1916. Portugal quickly mounted a large force and sent them bravely into battle in France. It seemed that the Portuguese knew this was potentially going to happen. In 1915, the nation had begun drafting soldiers into the army to build its ranks. Among these men was a humble farmer named Aníbal Milhais. This quiet young man was drafted into the Second Division and would eventually find himself deployed to France in 1917.

By April of 1918, Milhais' unit had seen nine months of action and was ready to be rotated out. Tired and emotionally drained, Aníbal and his platoon were prepared to go home and see their loved ones, but fate had different plans. The company had been taking heavy fire for days, and the Germans had moved their troops up in preparation for one last push (see Chapter 3: The Western Front - German Spring Offensive). The stage was set for a long and bloody battle, and Aníbal's units were smack dab in the middle of it. This battle would become known as the Battle of Lys.

Unfortunately, when the Battle of Lys started, Milhais and another soldier found themselves behind enemy lines. As the two of them sat at the bottom of a hill sheltering themselves from the artillery fire of the two previous days, gunshots rang out. The two soldiers climbed the hill they had been stuck behind trying to get to higher ground to see what was happening. As they topped the crest of the hill, they were greeted with a view of their battalion in full retreat. Knowing that they needed to make it back to their unit, the two Portuguese soldiers began their treacherous journey down the hill and back to their countrymen.

Along with the gunfire, the German soldiers were lobbing grenades into the retreating Portuguese troops. As Aníbal and his compatriot weaved through the broken landscape, one of those grenades landed near their path. The explosion was loud and tragically exploded close to the other soldier, killing him. To keep that from happening to him as well, Aníbal sheltered himself, and once the grenade explosions stopped, left the safety of his shelter only to find that the German forces had almost taken the hill he now stood on.

As he took in this sight, the Portuguese soldier knew that his brothers-in-arms would need more time to retreat. Reacting quickly to this unthinkable predicament, Aníbal stood up and reached for his Lewis machine gun. Standing on that hill, looking down at the fury of the German soldiers, he lifted his weapon and began firing. He moved from place to place on the hill, continually firing, hoping that the tactic would trick the Germans into believing that there were more soldiers than just him on that hill.

Feeling that the hill wasn't worth the loss of German soldiers, the German commander instructed his men to forget taking the hill and instead kept moving on their objective. Milhais would not stop, though; he continued firing on the enemy until he had no bullets left. The soldier found himself alone, behind enemy lines, with no ammunition. He knew that if he stayed in place, he was sure to be spotted, and so for three days, he kept on the move, hoping to find his way back to his unit eventually. On the third day, he stumbled upon a Scottish officer who had found himself in the same predicament, and together they found their way back to Allied territory.

Aníbal never spoke to anyone about what he had done, and his bravery would have gone unknown if not for a report filed by that Scottish officer. Aníbal would go on to earn several medals and return to his country a hero.

Ecaterina Teodoroiu

Born in a small village called Vădeni, young Ecaterina would have never guessed where life would lead her. Her fate would be far from what she dreamed. After four years of school, she moved on to a girl's school in Bucharest, where she studied to be a teacher. But in 1916, the Kingdom of Romania joined the war, and her destiny was written in stone. Course-correcting her life, she moved from preparing to become a teacher to serving her country, and that change in the path would leave her one of the greatest Romanian heroes of the war.

Over the years, Ecaterina had worked as both a scout and a nurse, and wanting to contribute to the effort, chose to use this experience on the front lines. The devoted patriot worked along with reserves forces and civilians at the Jiu River. Banding together, the Romanian troops stationed with her were able to hold the advancing German forces back. Charged with caring for the fallen soldiers, Ecaterina soon developed a respect for the level of patriotism that even the wounded had, and this patriotism was contagious. Tragedy would strike again, and fate would urge Ecaterina to course-correct. Word that her brother had fallen on the front line reached her, and this stirred the fire inside Ecaterina. The Romanian nurse chose a bold move for a woman at this time; she requested to be a front-line soldier. With reluctance, she was granted her wish and moved to the front to serve with the 18th Infantry Regiment.

Ecaterina was a smart woman, and because of this, she adapted to the strategic thinking of military life easily and quickly. This adaptability led her to assist in planning and to make some quick decisions when faced with difficult situations. For instance, at one point, her unit, surrounded by German soldiers, was in danger of being captured. With a quick wit and a masterful plan, she was able to fool the Germans and keep her comrades from being taken as prisoners.

Unfortunately, eventually, her smarts and tricks would run out, and she too would end up captured. It wouldn't be long before she began to formulate a plan to free herself from her German captives. Unbeknownst to the Germans, Ecaterina had managed to conceal a revolver from them. She waited for the perfect moment and then sprung on the soldiers guarding her. Fighting her way free, Ecaterina managed to get several shots and ended up killing two German soldiers. Finally free, she realized she had been hit, but it was a mere flesh wound, and she worked her way back to the front lines.

Over the next few days, Ecaterina's battalion would see plenty of combat, and eventually, Ecaterina would suffer an injury bad enough to take her off the battlefield. The injured soldier would be moved to a hospital in Iasi for a month while her wound healed. Once she was released, Ecaterina hurried back to the front line under the command of a new leader, Lieutenant Mănoiu. She would return not as a soldier, though, but as a nurse stationed with his infantry regiment. Her bravery even in this non-combatant role earned her many accolades, and eventually, she was made an Honorary Second Lieutenant and given command of a 25-man platoon.

Her battalion would see a lot of action as they moved their way closer to the front line. On August 17, as the battles became harsher and neared the end of the Romanian campaign, her commander asked her to stay behind at the mobile hospital. She refused and instead continued the move with her men.

Almost a month later, the Romanian lines were attacked by the Germans. While leading a counterstrike, Lieutenant Teodoroiu was struck in the chest or head—stories conflict—and she died on the battlefield.

Some say her final words were, "Forward men, I'm still with you!" The memory of Ecaterina Teodoroiu would live on and become a symbol of true Romanian patriotism and strength.

Edouard Izac

Edouard Izac was born to German immigrant parents in 1891 in Iowa. Being born to parents that spoke very little to no English meant that German was spoken in his home. So young Edouard was bilingual, which would be a good thing in the Spring of 1918. Izac would end up being a prisoner of war and use his knowledge of the German language to obtain information. Unfortunately for him, he was never able to use that knowledge as he would end up a prisoner for the remaining months of the war. But his heroic efforts and dedication to his country would be honored for decades to come.

Edouard Izac graduated from Annapolis in 1915 and was assigned to duty on the battleship *USS Florida*. Until the sinking of the *Lusitania* and the interception of the Zimmermann Telegram, it looked like the U.S. would be able to stay neutral through the war. However, with these two events, it was clear that the country could no longer avoid conflict. As the country geared up for a fight, the naval transport service needed new blood, and Izac was reassigned to the *USS President Lincoln*. This ship would be used to ferry American troops and equipment to the shores of Europe to aid the U.S. allies.

After several successful transports across the Atlantic, Izac was promoted to the ship's executive officer. Having just unloaded its fifth batch of troops, the ship was getting ready to turn around and return to the shores of the U.S. to pick up another load. The seas seemed calm as the boat entered open waters. But early the following morning, Lincoln's crew was shaken awake by massive vibrations that echoed through the bows of the ship. The ship had been struck from the side by three torpedoes from a hidden German U-boat. The crew rushed to the lifeboats and watched as the boat sunk rapidly. With the crew safely in the lifeboats, the leadership was unaware of the tragedy that was yet to come. Several feet away from the lifeboats, the U-boat that had sunk their ship surfaced.

The commander of the U-boat emerged, and escorted by his men demanded the *Lincoln*'s captain be turned over to prove to their commanders back home that they had sunk this ship. Izac, wanting to save his men from any further tragedy, stood up and told the German commander that their captain had gone down with the ship. With the captain dead, the Germans settled for the executive officer, and Izac was brought on board the submarine as a prisoner of war.

The Germans set Izac up with his own room and treated him with respect. But, unaware that Edouard spoke German, they also had no problem discussing sensitive material in front of him, and Izac soon realized this could be a significant advantage to the Allied war efforts. The sailor began listening intently and taking mental note of every little detail he thought could be used to aid his fellow soldiers once he escaped. Once the U-boat made its way back to their home base, Izac was moved to a POW camp.

While housed in this POW camp, Izac would not rest on his laurels. He knew he had information that was vital and needed to be delivered to the Allied commanders. So, he made several attempts to escape but failed every time. After being in that camp for a month, the German command decided that he needed to be moved to a new camp. Thinking this was a perfect moment, Izac attempted yet another escape. Midway through the transport, he made his move and was able to get away. Eventually, he was recaptured and beaten severely and taken on to the next camp. It was from this camp that he would make his final escape and find his way to Switzerland.

Unfortunately, he was unable to relay the critical information he had acquired during his time on the German submarine, as he found his way to the authorities on the very day that war ended, November 11, 1918. Though the delivery was too late, this sailor's stubbornness and desire to assist his country was truly heroic.

Chapter Five
Stories & Events

History is a series of moments and events; the stories within these moments are what bring that history to life, long after all is said and done. The stories of the Great War are many and full of epic battles, daring courage and heroic deeds that show the strength and the will of humanity.

There are so many stories to choose from and so much to be learned by studying them. After all, according to George Santayana, "Those who cannot remember the past are condemned to repeat it." These stories will allow you to remember what the people of that time were going through and how their strife and tragedy built the world we live in today.

The Sinking of the *Lusitania*

Many passenger ships would be commissioned to join the war efforts. The *Lusitania*, a British passenger ship, was one of these. It would still be used to transport passengers, but in 1914, would also be secretly modified to carry supplies and troops as well. By 1915, the German military command was well aware that British passenger ships were being used to ferry troops and arms across the Atlantic from the U.S. to the shores of the European continent to bolster the Allied efforts.

To the German naval commanders, this meant that these ships were fair game, and they had no problem making passenger and merchant ships targets of their U-boats. Knowing that America's interference would be a problem, the German embassy used the media outlets within the U.S. to help deter passengers from making the journey across the ocean. In 1915, a campaign was distributed in the U.S., warning the citizens that there was a war going on between the two European nations. That any person on one of the British passenger ships would then be an enemy of the German state, and they would be in danger of potential attacks. So, if the American public wanted to remain safe, they would avoid these ships at all costs.

These warnings fell on deaf ears as most assumed that the Germans would abide by common decency and allow any survivors to make it to lifeboats. Those assumptions turned out to be very wrong. Six days into the *Lusitania*'s voyage, in the early afternoon of May 7, off the coast of Ireland, the *Lusitania* was struck by a torpedo without any kind of warning, and quickly sank to the ocean floor.

The torpedo ripped through the bow of the passenger ship, opening up the hull, allowing tons of seawater to rush into the gaping hole rapidly. Within seconds of the initial strike, a secondary explosion rocked the ship, and this is what sealed the fate of the mighty ocean liner. In just 20 minutes, the boat was no longer visible. The ship sank so quickly that there was no time for many of the passengers or crew to escape to the lifeboats. Of the almost 2,000 people on board, approximately 760 survived. Even with this blatant disregard for human life, the Americans tried to maintain their neutrality.

There was outrage across the globe. Germany vehemently defended their actions by saying that the *Lusitania* carried weapons, which made it a war vessel, and therefore it was perfectly acceptable to take action against it. The media announcement of this outlandish claim only stirred up Britain's war propaganda machine. In the coming weeks, more British citizens headed to the recruiting stations to sign up to fight against the ruthless Germans. Along with this surge of patriotism, there came riots in the streets of London.

However, it would take more than one passenger ship sinking to get the U.S. to break their neutrality. Not long after the tragedy of the *Lusitania*, the Germans hit another vessel, and the U.S. knew they had to react with some sort of warning, so they cut off all diplomatic ties with Germany. With these two sinkings and the interception of the Zimmermann Telegram, there was no doubt that America's decision to declare war on Germany was justified and necessary.

The Christmas Truce

The war had been raging for five months (longer than most had predicted when it began), and the holiday season was coming quickly. So, to show goodwill to all men, a suggestion was issued from the walls of the Vatican. Pope Benedict XV wanted both sides to lay down their arms so that the birth of their savior could be celebrated without bloodshed. Neither side's leadership, though, took much notice of the papal suggestion. But as the stars began to shine on Christmas Eve, there were some signs that despite their commander's lack of support, the troops on both sides felt the same way.

Whether it was in response to the Pope's edict or just the soldiers missing their families and wanting a little reminder of them will never be known. As the breeze blew across the broken and corpse-filled fields, a noise began to waft across the fields. From the trenches on both sides of No Man's Land, Christmas carols began to ring out (some even accompanied by instruments according to some stories). The singing would continue into the late hours of the evening.

When the sun began to rise on Christmas Day, as the allied troops prepared for another long day of combat and tragedy, they began to hear distant murmurs that seemed like a familiar greeting. Over the distance, many of the soldiers thought they could hear someone wishing them a Merry Christmas. As they stuck their heads slowly over the trenches, German troops could be seen coming across No Man's Land, and as the enemy got closer, the Allied soldiers could more clearly make out the words, and it was the Merry Christmas that they had been hearing.

At first, the Allied soldiers thought that this could be a trick, but when the Germans got close enough, they could see that these troops were unarmed and genuinely wanted to have a day of celebration. With this realization, the Allied Forces began to emerge from their trenches as well—the soldiers, who, just days before, had been mercilessly killing each other, celebrated together.

The soldiers would do everything that they would typically do on Christmas morning. They exchanged gifts, played friendly soccer games, sang carols, and decorated trees. Though they didn't have much, they exchanged what they had, which meant things like cigarettes and even plum puddings. The day was filled with laughter and camaraderie.

With the cease-fire, some unfortunate tasks were also completed—things like retrieval of fallen soldiers from No Man's Land and treatment of unattended injuries. After a full day of camaraderie, the two sides returned to their trenches and prepared for the battle to begin again the next morning.

Japan Declares War

Just days after the British declared war on Germany, the British foreign secretary, looking to take advantage of an alliance agreement signed years before, reached out to the

Japanese leadership for help. Sir Edward Grey needed the Japanese to use their impressive navy to scout out German merchant ships that may be carrying supplies and weapons to the German forces. This request played right into the political aspiration of the Japanese as they wanted to expand their footprint in the Far East. Living up to their words in the 1902 Alliance Treaty, the Japanese acted swiftly, drawing a line in the sand with the German forces stationed at naval bases scattered throughout the Shantung Peninsula.

In August of 1914, the Japanese government forcefully suggested that the German military and merchant vessels remove themselves from Chinese and Japanese waters. With no word coming from the German commanders, the Japanese took that as a declaration of war and began to move their navy into a position to take Tsingtao immediately. The British, for their part, would help the Japanese by bolstering their already significant naval presence with two battalions of troops. By moving onto the German naval base at Tsingtao, they had lived up to their word and broken the neutrality of China.

Just a month after the Japanese troops landed and began their ground assault on the base in Tsingtao, the Germans surrendered. Though this may be the only major battle the

Japanese took part in during the war, it was a significant contribution to the war effort.

With the German forces removed from China, Russia would be free to focus their attention on its western border, instead of having to fight on another front like the Germans. Because of this defeat, the Japanese gained a foothold in China, a non-unified country, and were able to take control of not only the Shantung Peninsula but most of China, setting up this part of the world for decades of conflicts.

Zeppelin Raids

In 1900, Count Ferdinand Graf von Zeppelin came up with an idea for a new way to travel. This new mode of travel would be revolutionary and one that would come to be a tool used in Germany's war efforts to remove Britain from the equation. He had invented a giant flying ship that was filled with hydrogen to allow for flight and named it after himself, the Zeppelin.

It wouldn't take long for the German military to realize the advantage these vessels could lend them during wartime. After all, these vessels could travel 85 miles per hour and could haul about two tons of goods. The first test of this tool came over the skies of Antwerp and Paris. The missions in both cases showed great promise, and now the German leadership knew they had the means to get rid of the biggest thorn in their side, Britain. So, in January of 1915, the German government and military leadership moved their Zeppelin division in preparation for making their first move on to the mainland of England.

The giant ships were hard to hide, but the Germans knew that the payloads that they carried would deliver devastation no matter how much resistance they received from the British forces. So, the Zeppelins were deployed to the coastal cities of Yarmouth and Kings Lyn. The Germans hoped this would cause a panic and enhance the fear in England so much that they would pull their troops back to their shores and withdraw from the war. Attacking the coastal cities didn't seem to be doing the trick; the Germans knew where they had to attack. The hub of everything British would be the next big target. A little over four months after starting the initial Zeppelin raids, the mighty airships made their way to London.

On May 31, the Germans, guided by the lights of the Thames, moved one of their mighty Zeppelins through the skies over London. As the people of London drifted off to sleep, the German soldiers opened the trap door and began dropping their payload. The incendiary bombs and grenades silently plummeted through the pitch black, and seconds later, explosions rocked the city streets of the mighty British capital. The once darkened skies now lit up with the explosions and fires that rocked the sleeping city. Londoners were jostled or jumped from their beds; there were screams and shouts; the streets flooded with panicking people.

By the end of the first major raid on London, the Germans had dropped 890 bombs and 30 grenades. The attack was successful, and the Germans left triumphant, ready to use this tactic over and over again until the British relented. The success did not lie in the number of lives lost as they were light—seven dead, 35 wounded—rather in the fear and property damage that the English people had been subjected to on that fateful evening.

Zeppelin raids continued for the next few months using well-timed strikes to keep the British unnerved and on guard at all times. Eventually, the British would formulate ways to combat these flying death-dealers. The government instituted city-wide blackouts in the hopes that having no lights to guide them would hinder the Zeppelins' missions. Several significant sites and buildings were fitted with searchlights so that the Zeppelins could be spotted before they were able to attack. The police were also issued whistles that would act as air raid sirens to keep the sound of larger ones from being beacons for the Zeppelins to use to drop their devastation on the citizens of London.

These were mildly effective, but in 1916, the real game-changer made its appearance. Until that point, even though the British had planes (not many but some), none of them could fly high enough to reach the Zeppelins. To fix this problem, the British engineers had begun mounting guns on the newly manufactured planes. These guns shot bullets that could break through the Zeppelin balloon, which would ignite the hydrogen used for flight.

Though the British had unveiled this new very effective countermeasure, the Germans would continue trying this technique well into 1917, but finally realizing that the Zeppelins were no longer as effective as they were, they would move on to a new technique. This new method of attack would be more maneuverable and less noticeable; the Germans would begin using bombers to devastating effectiveness.

Churchill Steps Down

The Battle of Gallipoli led to the death of many Allied troops and did not yield the territory or strategic gain that was expected. The campaign was riddled with incompetent leadership and poor execution, both in the timing as well as the maneuvers.

Unfortunately, the weight of these failures fell squarely on one man's shoulder: Winston Churchill. Long before he was the British Bulldog and led his country to victory during WWII, Churchill had many enemies due to his more liberal and imperialist leanings. Because of his political ideology, stubbornness, and mishandling of the Gallipoli Campaign, he soon found himself demoted to a cabinet post that no one had even heard of before. After the Dardanelles debacle, the conservatives wanted him out of the admiralty, and they got their wish.

Churchill, feeling slighted and unfairly targeted as the person who had let this opportunity slip through the hands of the British forces, resigned from office. Instead of standing in the parliament, he opted to join the rest of the British troops on the front line.

He gained a commission into the British Expeditionary Forces and ended up in France. Serving with the Royal Scots Fusiliers, Churchill would have many close calls and eventually make his way back home in 1917. With his return, he set his eye on a political resurrection. The liberal politician would serve the war effort in a wholly different manner as he was appointed to be the Minister of Munitions in a very progressive government headed by Prime Minister David Lloyd George. Here, he would work his way up and eventually be elected Prime Minister of Britain in 1940.

Conclusion

Sensing the end was near, U.S. President Woodrow Wilson stood before Congress early in 1918 and laid out his vision of what the post-war world would entail. This vision was comprised of 14 points aimed at maintaining peace in Europe and the rest of the world. Wilson predicted a victory for the Allies and said it would be up to them to set the terms of peace but do so with unselfish aims and greedy machinations. Things like international waters, restoration of occupied land, and the ability of nations to self-govern themselves all found a home in the 14 points of Wilson's speech.

By the fall of 1918, both sides showed the signs of the long and arduous four years of war. The Central Powers had taken a beating with major offensives like the Hundred Day Offensive. The rise of disease, starvation, and the conflict itself had wiped out much of both armies. However, the

Allied Forces had more ability to bring fresh troops to the front, and this meant that the Germans were severely outnumbered. One by one, the allies of the Central Powers began to fall to the Allied Forces, and as each fell, it became more and more evident that the war was coming to an end.

In October, both members of the Central Powers asked the U.S. president to begin talks for a truce. Both nations had heard Wilson's address to the U.S. Congress at the beginning of the year and felt that the points he relayed were fair. In fact, the armistice and subsequent treaty would contain a majority of the ideas expressed by Wilson.

On November 3, the Austro-Hungarian Empire would be dealt a crushing defeat at Trieste, and here, they would sign their armistice, bringing the war on the eastern front to an end. Four days later, in a railway carriage (which would play a role in the next Great War as well when Hitler took Paris) at Compiegne, the Germans and the Allies sat down to begin negotiations for their armistice. (Two days later, Kaiser Wilhelm II abdicated his throne and fled to the Netherlands.)

The German leaders came to the table, expecting a word-for-word document of President Wilson's plan, but instead, they met that, plus two significant stipulations added. They would not only have to pay reparations, but lands that had been gained plus some would be returned or ceded to the nations affected by the war. All the points discussed at this meeting would find their way to the Treaty of Versailles, the final ruling on the matter, and the peace accord that would appease the Allied Forces.

With the outline for the treaty laid out, all parties would gather again for the final signing. The final signing would take place in Paris and be led by the leaders of the big four nations—the U.S., Britain, France, and Italy. At the Paris Peace Conference, the final figures and stipulations would be hammered out.

The defeated nations attended the summit. They had been the instigators and, therefore, much like criminals in a trial, had no say over their punishment. The terms decided by the four major nations of the Allied Forces were presented in front of both German and Austro-Hungarian representatives. Though the severity of the conditions impacted both countries, Germany was hit the hardest. Germany would lose territory and ten percent of its population through the committee's redrawing of the nation's borders in eastern and western Europe. (The Middle East would be affected as well. Here, the redrawing of boundaries would set the Middle East up for decades of perpetual conflict.) Since Germany had been deemed the aggressor, they were solely responsible for all the reparations. In the end, this war ended up costing the German state and people roughly 33 million U.S. Dollars, which was to be repaid over the coming decades.

The severity of the terms was determined to be the only way to make sure that Germany would never be a threat again to the people of Europe and the world (it would have the opposite effect).

To drive this point home, the agreement also restricted the German military to only having 100,000 men and created a demilitarized zone in the Rhineland area of Western Germany.

German dignitaries protested against some of the new additions, saying that they were not part of the 14 points they had agreed to when beginning the peace talks. However, in the end, all the additional rules and terms were reluctantly accepted. With the final draft completed, the parties once again met. This time at the Palace of Versailles and on June 28, 1919, the Treaty of Versailles was signed.

The signing of the treaty changed the world forever. From it, new nations formed, current countries were expanded, and the world governing body, the League of Nations, was created. This precursor of the United Nations would be the international governing body for almost three decades until finally being replaced with a more impressive and effective organization. The league had some wins but also succumbed to the self-interest of the more wealthy and powerful nations more often than not.

The ramifications of the Great War would ripple throughout the world for decades to come. Many historians criticize the Treaty of Versailles for its roles in creating more tensions. Of all the ramifications of the treaty, many feel the one that had the most significant impact on the future was the harsh terms placed on Germany.

These terms would lead to economic hardship, unemployment, and, eventually, a recession. These consequences of the terms of the treaty would lead to the rise of a powerful and very dangerous nationalist leader, Adolf Hitler, who would lead Germany into another war on the global stage just a few decades later.

Trivia Questions & Answers

History Student

Why was Archduke Ferdinand assassinated?

Answer: Serbian nationalists that opposed the rule of the Austro-Hungarian Empire over Bosnia wanted freedom and control of their own country. So, on June 28, 1914, Gavrilo Princip fired the shots that would kill the archduke and his wife, beginning the first world war.

Where was the first major battle of World War I?

Answer: The first major battle of WWI took place at Marne and lasted from September 6-10, 1914. This site is located in the northwest of France, about 50 miles from Paris.

The war lasted a lot longer than the parties involved had anticipated, so that meant more men would have to join

to keep the forces stocked. **How many people would enlist in total?**

Answer: Over the four years that the battle raged, 65 million individuals from both sides would join the fight.

Both sides had their coalition names. On one side, you had the Central Powers, and on the other, you had the Allied Powers. Three countries that were part of the Allied Forces were also known under another name. What was that name?

Answer: The three-country unit was known as the Triple Entente.

Which countries were a part of the Triple Entente?

Answer: The UK, France, and Russia. (By the way, the Central Powers were also known as the Triple Alliance and consisted of Germany, Italy, and Austria-Hungary.)

The war would eventually be taken up by a majority of the powers of the world, but who declared war first?

Answer: After the assassination of the Austro-Hungarian heir in Sarajevo, the first declaration came from the Austro-Hungarian empire.

There were few places more dangerous in WWI than the area between the trenches. It was so deadly that troops came up with a name for it. What did the soldiers call that area?

Answer: The name didn't have to be smart, just accurate. Soldiers called it "No Man's Land."

As a result of the war ending, a mighty governing body formed to make sure a conflict of this magnitude wouldn't happen again. What was the name of this group?

Answer: After the Treaty of Versailles, a global ruling organization known as the League of Nations was formed. This governing body was invented to keep things like war from happening.

How long was the League of Nations active?

Answer: The League of Nations would be active from 1919 until 1946. At this point, it dissolved, and the UN filled its place in the world.

Many factors led the world to war, but these main political concepts played the most prominent roles. What

were the three movements that helped bring the world to the precipice of war?

Answer: The three social and political movements were imperialism, militarism, and nationalism.

Once the Bolsheviks took charge in Russia, the leader of that party felt it was time to pull his troops back from the eastern front of the war. Which leader made this decision?

Answer: In 1917, Lenin began to pull the Russian troops back to the mother country as he looked to start building a communist nation and wanted to have all his people there to help him do it. There were remnants of the White Army that needed to be taken care of before the new government could be formed as well.

The truce stopped the fighting on what day in history?

Answer: The truce was the first step in ending the war and went into effect on November 11, 1918. It would be a couple of months before the actual treaty would be signed, but this was a good start in ending the bloodshed.

When talking about the causes of the war, many people use the acronym MAIN. What does it stand for?

Answer: It stands for militarism, alliances, imperialism, and nationalism.

What neutral country did Germany march through at the beginning of the war?

Answer: Germany's move was intended to be in France, but before they got to France, they had to march through Belgium. This country had been neutral, and once Germany began mobilizing through its land, Britain soon realized they would be needed in the effort to stop Germany's aggression.

Why did Germany decide to attack both France and Russia?

Answer: It was all about alliances. The Russians did not support Austria-Hungary's annexation of Serbia and instead backed the Serbian nationalists. After this decision, Russia became enemies with Austria-Hungary, who had a strong alliance with Germany. So, the minute the Russian troops moved to the border, Germany moved to help their ally out. Russia also had an agreement with France, and the German leadership knew that once Germany and Austria-Hungary moved on Russia, the French were obliged to send troops to help their comrades out. So as a stop-gap measure, the Germans sent troops to cut off the French's capability to send their troops. This led to Germany ending up fighting a two-front war.

Which country did Germany declare war on first, Russia or France?

Answer: Germany declared war on Russia first. On August 1, 1914, Germany would make the pronouncement that they would be going to war with Russia. Two days later, on August 3, 1914, they extended the same proclamation to France.

When did the British Expeditionary Force (BEF) land in France?

Answer: The BEF first set foot on French soil on August 7, 1914. Though smaller than the French Army, the British forces were better trained.

Turkey would join the war after it had already begun. When did they enter the war, and on what side?

Answer: Turkey and the Ottoman Empire had signed into a treaty in 1914, with Germany as the newly-formed German State that helped them greatly with their military building efforts. On October 29, 1914, Turkey would join the war efforts on the side of Germany. Turkey felt they had to help and that by joining in with the German efforts, they could potentially destabilize the control of the French and British in other Muslim countries.

The Battle of the Falkland Islands was a significant win for the British naval forces. What date did this battle occur?

Answer: The Battle of the Falkland Islands took place on December 8, 1914.

And how many German and British soldiers were lost at the Battle of the Falkland Islands?

Answer: This battle was a decisive victory, where the British only lost ten men, whereas the Germans lost 2,000 men.

The *Lusitania* was a passenger ship that was sunk and played a significant role in the U.S. joining the war. Where was it sunk?

Answer: On May 7, 1915, the *RMS Lusitania* was attacked by the German U-boat *U-28* off the southern coast of Ireland.

How many people were lost when the *Lusitania* sank?

Answer: When the ship sank, 1,198 passengers went down with it, 100 of those being citizens of America.

When and why did Kaiser Wilhelm II abdicate the German throne?

Answer: There was a wide swath of unrest spreading across the German state. With a naval mutiny having just been executed and that growing unrest, the political leaders of Germany were convinced to push for the abdication. So, on November 9, 1918, Kaiser Wilhelm II left the throne and fled to the Netherlands.

What was the name of the general of the French Sixth Army that led the troops to success at the First Battle of Marne?

Answer: General Michel-Joseph Maunoury led the Sixth Army Division. This wartime hero had been retired for several years when the French Army called him back to service. In August of 1914, the 67-year-old artillery officer would find his way back to the battlefield and lead the Sixth Army to victory in the First Battle of Marne.

After being driven back, where did the German Army retreat after the First Battle of Marne?

Answer: The battle pushed the German forces back to the northern edge of the Aisne River.

The defeat at the Battle of Marne set into motion a series of flanking maneuvers on both sides. What were these maneuvers called?

Answer: "Race to the Sea." When the Germans retreated to the Aisne river, they began trying to use trenches to outflank their enemy. To counteract this, the other side started doing this themselves. This back and forth led to a series of trenches all linked together and protected at the top by barb wire, which was the real beginning of trench warfare during WWI.

What was the German Army's big mistake at the Battle of Marne?

Answer: The leader of the German forces moved his troops in the wrong direction. This maneuver created a hole in the German defensive line and allowed the French and British to separate the forces, weakening their ability to fight effectively.

And who was the leader that made the mistake?

Answer: The breach in the German Army line came when General Alexander von Kluck moved his troops north instead of west.

What were some of the reasons for the German defeat at the First Battle of Marne?

Answer: There were many reasons that the German Army wasn't at full strength, starting with the movement of 11 different divisions away from the line looking to advance and take over Paris. These divisions dispersed to other areas like Belgium and East Prussia as reinforcement for the conflicts going on in these regions. The German Army had also marched 150 miles without stopping, and the troops were exhausted. While they marched, they also saw many battles, which led to fatigue. The French Army was also not taking any chances and had begun demolishing bridges and railways, so that would mean fewer supplies as well as further to travel for the Germans. The Germans underestimated the French, which was a severe tactical miscalculation.

When was the First Battle of Marne fought?

Answer: The battle began in northeastern France, just 30 miles from Paris on September 6, 1914. Within the six days of the First Battle of Marne, the world would see many casualties and introduce some innovations. The battle would come to an end on September 12, 1914.

How many ships and sailors participated in the historic naval Battle at Jutland?

Answer: Altogether, there were over 250 ships and 100,000 sailors involved in the epic military Battle at Jutland.

Where was the Battle of Jutland?

Answer: The Battle of Jutland was the most massive naval battle in history and took place off the North Sea coast of Denmark.

When did the Battle of Jutland start and end?

Answer: The battle began on May 31, 1916, and ended just one day later on June 1, 1916.

Who were the admirals on each side of the Battle of Jutland?

Answer: Admiral John Jellicoe commanded the British fleet that saw action in the Battle of Jutland. For the opposition, the German fleet was led by Admiral Reinhard Scheer.

When did the Battle of Verdun take place?

Answer: The first barrage of German artillery began on February 21, 1916. The battle would last for almost a year and finally came to its conclusion on December 18, 1916.

How many casualties were there on each side?

Answer: Though the numbers are not wholly accurate, the estimate of lives lost in the 11-month battle comes to 400,000 on the French side and 350,000 on the German side.

Who was the German general who lead the Spring Offensive?

Answer: The German mastermind behind the Spring Offensive was General Erich Ludendorff.

How significant was the battlefront of the Spring Offensive?

Answer: Ludendorff chose a large swath of land to execute his Spring Offensive. A total of approximately 50 miles of the western front's Allied defense line would be the German's last great push.

What were the two goals that General Ludendorff had for the Spring Offensive?

Answer: Ludendorff intended to use psychological warfare and tactics to eliminate the British part of the resistance army. To do this, the central part of the plan was to drive the German Army between the French and British troops. Then turn north to deal with the less experienced British Army, thereby eliminating the French reinforcements.

Who was the French commander at the Battle of Amiens?

Answer: The man who spearheaded the Battle of Amiens for the French was General Ferdinand Foch.

What nations played a role in the Battle of Amiens as part of the Fourth Army?

Answer: To bolster Rawlinson's Army, he added infantry divisions from Britain, Canada, Australia, and America.

The Gallipoli Campaign, like all other battles, has been called many things. What are two different names for this tragic Allied loss?

Answer: This campaign is also known as the Battle of Gallipoli and the Dardanelles Campaign.

What does ANZAC stand for?

Answer: One of the pivotal forces in the execution of the Gallipoli Campaign was the ANZACs. This force was the Australian and New Zealand Army Corps – ANZAC.

What was the main objective of the Gallipoli Campaign?

Answer: Gallipoli was undertaken after Grand Duke Nicholas asked for help. The British naval command had reason to execute a campaign they had wanted to do for years. Not only would they be helping their Russian allies, but they would also be able to control the sea route from Europe to Russia.

Why did the Russian Grand Duke Nicholas ask for help from Britain in 1915?

Answer: The Russians needed a way to end the involvement of the Turkish forces in the Caucus Mountain area so they would only have to fight foes on one side.

What were the two beachheads established by the Allied Forces on the Gallipoli Peninsula?

Answer: The beachhead established on the southern tip of the peninsula was called Helles. Though later it would be renamed in honor of the fallen ANZAC soldiers, ANZAC

Cove. The second beachhead was on the Aegean, and it was called Gaba Tepe.

When was the evacuation of Gallipoli ordered?

Answer: The initial order to begin evacuation came down on December 7, 1915.

How long did the evacuation take to complete?

Answer: The last troops did not leave until January 9, 1916.

What were the results of the Battle of Megiddo for the Ottoman forces and Empire?

Answer: The Ottoman's loss at Megiddo sealed the fate of the 600-year reign of this mighty empire. They were forced to sign an armistice on October 30. In this armistice, they agreed to the partition of their empire, giving lands back to previously-conquered places. Though it would take a few years for the final dissolution of empire (it wouldn't be until 1923, until it officially ended) altogether, this indeed was the final blow.

Where and when did the "Red Baron" die?

Answer: The "Red Baron" had been given his fighting squadron and was engaging the enemy in April 1918. As he swooped low to follow an enemy plane, he was taken by surprise by a machine gunner on the ground. He would take a bullet and lose control of his plane, nose-diving into the ground and meeting his end.

Who was Edith Cavell?

Answer: Edith Cavell, a British nurse, formerly from the Norfolk area of England, became a hero to the Belgian Resistance. She helped Allied troops escape occupied-Belgium through a path to the neutral Netherlands and back to England.

Where was the *Lusitania* bound for when it launched?

Answer: The *Lusitania* launched from Liverpool and was headed to New York.

What former president of the U.S. demanded retaliation after the sinking of the *Lusitania*?

Answer: Woodrow Wilson decided not to instigate any ill feelings with the German state when this happened, but former President Teddy Roosevelt felt this was not the right move and called for immediate retaliation for the American lives lost.

When was the first Zeppelin raid on London executed?

Answer: On May 31, 1915, the Germans used the Thames River and its lights to guide them toward their most significant target yet, London. The doors opened that night and dropped 90 incendiary bombs and 30 grenades onto the unsuspecting people of London.

History Buff

War is deadly, but there was another fatal enemy during the war. What caused a third of the military deaths during the war?

Answer: It wasn't bullets or tanks. No, the outbreak of the Spanish Influenza took its toll on the military men and women of the Great War. There were three primary outbreaks, two of which were during the war.

What well-known moniker did the German pilot, Manfred von Richthofen, go by?

Answer: The illustrious German pilot is better known as the Red Baron.

How many enemy planes did he shoot down?

Answer: In his flying career, he shot down a whopping 80 British and French planes.

Which general led the American Army on the western front?

Answer: General John "Black Jack" Pershing was the commander of the American Expeditionary Forces (AEF) that fought alongside the French and British troops to fend off the advancing German empire.

World War I was known by a few different names. What were the two main ones?

Answer: The war would be dubbed World War I, but it was also known as "The War to End All Wars" and "The Kaiser's War."

The U.S. tried to keep from entering the war, but eventually, they would see that they needed to help their allies. What was the date the U.S. finally joined the conflict?

Answer: At first, President Wilson stated that the U.S. would stay neutral in the conflict. However, Germany's announcement that they were going to use submarines without prejudice to keep merchant ships from entering Britain became a problem. This decree would lead to the sinking of the *Lusitania*, which had 128 American citizens on board. On top of that, the "Zimmermann Telegram" was intercepted, and its content threatened U.S. borders. This telegraph insinuated that Germany would ally with Mexico. At that point, Wilson had no alternative, and he sent America to the war on April 6, 1917.

Russia fought a two-sided war while the war ensued. On their western border, they were crucial components in the World War, but in 1917, they also began to experience their internal conflict. What was this conflict?

Answer: In 1917, after two separate revolutions occurred, the people overthrew the aristocracy and put the Bolsheviks in power. With that, the USSR was born.

What caused the political upheaval in Russia?

Answer: The people of Russia had enough of their Tsars and their lavish lives. They starved and struggled while the Tsars kept making decisions that only impacted them.

Tanks played a role in combat for the first time during WWI. What was the prototype tank called?

Answer: In 1915, the UK's Landship Committee began building a weapon that was intended to turn the tides. Dubbed the *Little Willie*, after months of designing and manufacturing, the tank made its way to combat in August of that same year.

Germany's decision to attack two fronts was a controversial one. In what document was this plan outlined?

Answer: Germany intended to attack the French on one side and the Russians on the other. The Schlieffen Plan would lay this plan out in detail.

Trench warfare was new, so there was a cost unknown other than the artillery and gunfire. The soldiers in the trenches experienced many medical conditions. Name two different ailments they struggled with.

Answer: Two medical ailments have been given their name for their extensive proliferation during the Great War. The first and most common was the Trench Foot. This condition was caused by long periods of exposure to dampness, cold, and unsanitary conditions. Many of the men were stuck in trenches, no matter the weather and without access to dry clothes. Because of this, they would end up with trench foot, which could lead to amputation in severe circumstances. The other ailment was known as Trench Mouth. This disease was a severe form of necrotic gingivitis. It was contracted by not having access to hygiene tools and exposure to unsanitary situations like the trenches of WWI.

The first battle of the eastern front was the Battle of Tannenberg. Why was it so important other than it is the first battle?

Answer: For the Central Powers, this battle showed the weakness of the Russian Army. This battle would lead Germany and its allies to be emboldened and put a little more effort into fighting on the eastern front. (Though most of the focus was still on the western front.)

After America joined the battle, there were a lot of open jobs. Because of this, a lot of African Americans moved to the north to fill these positions. What was this called?

Answer: Not long removed from the end of the civil war and still under the oppression of Jim Crow laws, the blacks of the south wanted to escape the systematic racism of the south. With the mass opening of jobs due to the war efforts, there was a need for workers, so the Great Migration began.

To have enough soldiers to send into battle, President Wilson and Congress enacted what act?

Answer: When the U.S. decided to help their allies out, they were not suited for conflict of this size, so they needed a way to get a ton of men into the service. On May 18, 1917, the Selective Service Act was passed. The law would give the president the power to draft non-disabled men into the military.

To keep the public from panicking and help prevent protests, the U.S. government passed an act that would make it illegal to criticize the government in publications or by individuals. What was the act called?

Answer: The act was called the Sedition Act.

When did the Sedition Act go into effect?

Answer: The bill was signed into law in April of 1917, just a few weeks after Wilson decreed war.

War is a pricey endeavor, and when America joined the cause, they did not have enough to fund the war. So what actions were taken to help with this problem?

Answer: To absorb some of the costs, the U.S. government instituted an income tax, war profits tax, and an excise tax. Along with the placement of taxes on this fund, the government also began selling government bonds.

Who was the commander of the Austro-Hungarian armies?

Answer: Franz Conrad von Hötzendorf led the Austro-Hungarian Armies.

What did Charles Whittlesey use to stop the friendly fire from bombarding his troop's position?

Answer: During the battle in the Argonne Forest, Whittlesey and his troops (which would later become known as the Lost Battalion) were trapped, surrounded by enemy forces. During the battle, his battalion would begin taking fire from the Allies, and he would use a carrier pigeon to send a message, letting the Allies know that their artillery was falling on comrades.

How many German soldiers did Alvin York and his unit capture?

Answer: During the famous battle of the Meuse-Argonne Offensive on October 8, 1918, Sergeant York and the men of the 82nd Division would capture 132 German soldiers.

What was the name of the U.S. aviation hero that was known by the nickname "The Balloon Buster"?

Answer: In a single week, Frank Luke took down 14 enemy aviators. Ten of those were surveillance balloons aimed at relaying tactical locations and troop movements to the German Army. For this amazing and heroic feat, the pilot was soon dubbed "The Balloon Buster."

The German aviation corps had the Red Baron, but what U.S. aviator had the most victories?

Answer: The most famous American flying ace of WWI was Second Lieutenant Eddie Rickenbacker. In his flying carrier, the pilot shot down 26 enemies, 22 planes, and four balloons.

How old was the youngest soldier to receive a Victoria Cross?

Answer: This honor would go to a young man who stuck to his post even after being fatally wounded. First Class Jahn Cromwell would receive this honor at the very young age of 16.

How many Victoria Crosses were awarded during and for actions taken in World War I?

Answer: Roughly 634 were awarded for bravery and acts of heroism in the face of extreme danger.

Everyone knows about the Red Baron, but there was another famous German flying ace that was a hero to his people. What was his name, and how many enemy planes did he shoot down?

Answer: The runner-up in the German aviation corps was Ernst Udet. This pilot would work throughout the war and shoot down a total of 61 enemy planes.

Just a year after the war began, Russia's ruler took control of the reigns of the army. When did he do this?

Answer: To reinvigorate his army, Tsar Nicholas II would take complete control over the Russian military on September 5, 1915.

To make sure that the BEF had enough recruits to fight the war, the government instituted conscription. When did this go into effect?

Answer: The British government activated the conscription ruling on January 27, 1916.

Getting your soldiers and weapons behind enemy objects is always a play when in the midst of war. Germans were able to get a U-Boat in U.S. waters during the war. What U-boat was this and when did it arrive in U.S. waters?

Answer: This was the first enemy vessel in U.S. waters since 1812. The German U-boat, *U-151*, entered the waters on the east coast with the mission of laying mines and cutting underwater telegraph lines. The submarine entered these waters on May 25, 1918.

After the First Battle of Marne, the war would be fought in the trenches, but that wasn't the only warfare that this conflict saw. There were two military tactics used that had never been used before: what were they?

Answer: Part of the reason the conflict at Marne was so successful was due to air surveillance, but this would not have been so effective without the radio intercepts. Airplanes were relatively new to combat, and being able to receive an audio transmission on troop movements leveled the playing field a bit a more. Along with radio intercepts, the use of the "Marne taxis" was the first use of the automotive transport of troops. Before this, it would have taken days for the soldiers to arrive to replenish the French Army. Going forward, these two military tactics would become the norm.

What advantages did the British fleet have over the German Navy?

Answer: The most significant advantage was the number of ships. In comparison to the German fleet, the British had 37 heavy vessels versus the Germans' 27 boats. For the smaller vessels, the British had 113 versus the Germans' 72. On top of the advantage of having more ships, they also cracked the German signal codes early, which allowed them to maneuver to counteract the Germans' tactical movements and brace for any potential attacks.

How did Vice Admiral Beatty lose three ships in the initial skirmishes of the Battle of Jutland?

Answer: These three battleships were not equipped with anti-flash protection. This flaw in their design meant that when shelled by the German fleet, the fire was able to make it into the powder houses. In turn, this caused massive explosions, damaging the ships enough that they would end up sinking or very damaged that they were useless to the naval efforts.

What time did the second phase of the Battle of Jutland start?

Answer: At 7:15 on the evening of May 31, the German fleet ran into the Grand Fleet.

What was the opening maneuver of the Battle of Jutland?

Answer: To form a blockade, the British ships wheeled to port 90 degrees. This maneuver prevented the German fleet from reaching their home port to recoup their losses.

How did the German fleet escape?

Answer: Admiral Scheer, knowing the battle and the fleet may well be lost if he couldn't retreat, had his ships do three separate 180-degree turns. This maneuver allowed the fleet to elude the tactics of their enemy and find a way to get back to Wilhelmshaven to recoup. In this battle, both sides took significant damage.

How many men and tons were lost in this battle?

Answer: The British lost approximately 6,784 men and 111,000 tons. In comparison, the Germans lost 3,050 men and 62,000 tons.

How did the Battle of Jutland change the German naval strategy during WWI?

Answer: The superiority of the British fleet was evident, so they course-corrected and began an attack on the British economy. This decision meant using their ships and U-Boats to attack commercial vessels.

Why did the German military strategists feel that Verdun was an excellent place to execute this attack?

Answer: The Germans were looking for a bastion of French pride, one that would drive the French to throw their soldiers onto the battle, no matter the cost. It also didn't hurt that the citadel was threatening the efficiency of the German communications line.

Who commanded a vital army division in the field and on the ground for the German forces?

Answer: Though the chief commander was General Erich von Falkenhayn, the ground soldiers of the Fifth Army were led by Crown Prince Wilhelm, who was the current Kaiser's eldest son.

How did the French come to be alerted to the German movement in the Verdun region?

Answer: In January, French reconnaissance planes noticed a strange surge of German troops along the area. However, it wasn't until February that French intelligence reported back to command of the forces amassing on the right bank of the Meuse River.

How long was the motorized supply train, and how many vehicles were in the convoy executed by the French for the Battle of Verdun?

Answer: The motorized supply train used for the first time in warfare to help the French stay supplied with both equipment and men drove down a 37-mile stretch of road. On this dirt road, about 3,000 trucks would travel, loaded down with the essentials to keep the front lines replenished and reinforced.

What was the road called?

Answer: The road would come to be known as the La Voie Sacrée or the Sacred Way.

Who was the leader of the French forces at Verdun?

Answer: At the beginning of the Battle of Verdun, the French High Command felt that there could be no better leader than the "Victor of Marne," General Joseph Jacques Césaire Joffre.

Who later replaced him, and why?

Answer: In May, after several defeats, the high command had lost faith in Joffre and decided to replace him with General Philippe Pétain.

How many shells did the Germans unleash at the initial artillery strike of the Battle of Verdun, and how long did it last?

Answer: The opening salvo of the Battle of Verdun took eight hours, and the German artillery launched approximately two million shells onto the French defensive line.

How many divisions did the German and Allies have at their disposal for the German Spring Offensive of 1918?

Answer: In preparation for the Spring Offensive, the Germans upped their presence on the western front. That left the German Army with 191 divisions available for combat during the Spring Offensive. For the Allies, they only had access to 178 divisions.

What was the code name given by Ludendorff to the first wave of the Spring Offensive?

Answer: The German code name for the opening skirmish of the Spring Offensive was Michael.

When was the opening salvo executed?

Answer: The Spring Offensive would launch on March 21, 1918, and would do so with a five-hour bombardment of the French defensive line.

How many mortars were used?

Answer: During this battle, 6,473 bullets would be fired as well as 3,532 mortars were lobed into that defensive line.

What two factors gave the Allies an advantage at the Battle of Amiens?

Answer: The advantages that made a huge difference were all types of deception. The first came backed by bogus communication. The Allies moved troops from the front lines to make it seem as though defenses were waning. In truth, the armies had been reinforced with nightly troop movements by other members of the Allied coalition. The Allies also used smoke screens as they began their push into German territory. The smoke gave them a tactical advantage over the weakened and demoralized German Army.

What hampered the success of the Gallipoli Campaign?

Answer: There was one main problem that kept the British forces from being successful in executing the Gallipoli Campaign. The first was a lack of intelligence on the people or the terrain. This lack of understanding of the ground, as well as the level of Turkish resistance, helped keep the British and their allies perpetually off-kilter as they went about executing their plans.

What two bodies of water connect via the Dardanelles?

Answer: The Dardanelles connected the Aegean Sea with the Marmara Sea.

Why was the strait important?

Answer: By taking this strait, it would have allowed the Allied Forces to safely transport supplies and troops through the strait to reinforce the Russian forces. This would help the Russian troops to stave off the advances of the Ottoman Empire.

Who was one of the British leaders who led the naval attack on the Dardanelles?

Answer: There were several leaders during this battle, but one of the top guys was First Lord of the British Admiralty, Winston Churchill. Churchill would bear the brunt of the fault for the unsuccessful campaign and would be demoted, eventually resigning altogether, and joining the front lines as a soldier. He, of course, would go on to become one of the most important men in the world and the leader of his nation during the next Great War.

After the first wave of attack, the naval battle was unsuccessful at Gallipoli; what happened?

Answer: After the initial failed naval attack, the British regrouped and planned a land attack instead that would be backed by naval vessels.

How many casualties were there on both sides during the Gallipoli Campaign?

Answer: Altogether, the casualties would tally about 500,000. Both sides experienced about 250,000 losses. Of those 250,000 casualties for the Allies, there were approximately 46,000 who lost their lives. On the Ottoman side, they experienced roughly 250,000 losses, of which 65,000 were deaths.

The Turkish resistance forces were led by a man that would later become a Turkish hero. What name does most of the world know Mustafa Kemal?

Answer: Mustafa Kemal was an imposing figure and one that had a deep sense of pride in his country. He would later go on to lead the way for the Turkish Republic after the Ottoman Empire was dissolved and would come to be known by the name Atatürk.

What happened to Churchill after the loss at Gallipoli?

Answer: He was initially demoted to an obscure cabinet position. Feeling slighted and a little by the fact that he was the scapegoat, he resigned and fought on the front lines with the Royal Scot Fusiliers. He would return to politics in 1917, and become the Minister of Munitions, and the rest of his career is, as they say, history.

There were a lot of transitions after the Battle for the Gallipoli Peninsula failed, even the British Prime Minister. Who took over after H.H. Asquith resigned his post?

Answer: A liberal government took hold after Asquith resigned and was led by David Lloyd George.

What was the Turkish name of the Gallipoli Campaign?

Answer: The Turkish call the campaign the Battle of Çanakkale.

What was one of the reasons that the Ottoman Empire joined the war?

Answer: Besides the fact they had an alliance with Germany, the Ottomans also thought that when the Central Powers won, they would regain control over the land they had previously ruled over. Places like Egypt and the Balkans were top of their list.

What two battles made up the Battle of Megiddo?

Answer: The two battles were the Battle of Sharon and the Battle of Nablus.

When was the Battle of Sharon?

Answer: On September 19, 1918, the initial battle of what would come to be called the Battle of Megiddo started.

When was Baron Richthofen (the Red Baron) born, and where?

Answer: Baron Manfred von Richthofen, the man known as the Red Baron, was born May 2, 1892, in Prussia—to be exact, what is now known as Breslau, Germany.

Baron Richthofen was born into a high-class family, and military service was expected. How old was Richthofen when he enrolled in military school?

Answer: Young Richthofen spent his early youth hunting and playing sports, but when he turned 11, that all came to a stop as he began his career path to military success.

When was the "Red Baron's" first victory logged?

Answer: The flying ace's first victory was on September 17, 1916.

Where was it, and who did he shoot down?

Answer: It was over France. There was a battle; he was able to shoot down a British fighter.

What medal did Richthofen earn when he collected his first 16 victories?

Answer: The medal was known as the Blue Max by the public, but its official name was the Pour le Mérite.

What was the name of the squadron that Richthofen was given command of?

Answer: Officially, the name of the unit was Jasta 11. However, because the pilots of this squadron painted their planes in bright colors and were able to do crazy aerial maneuvers, they became known as "The Flying Circus."

How many men did Cavell help get back to the safety of Allied territory?

Answer: The numbers are not definitive, but most reports say that she helped approximately 200 soldiers before being captured by the Germans.

When was Cavell arrested?

Answer: The Germans had kept a close eye on Cavell with spies and consistent inspections of her facility. Eventually, her extracurricular activities were detected, and in August of 1915, she was arrested and held for trial.

When was Cavell court-martialed?

Answer: She was arrested in August, but it wasn't until October 2 that she was court-martialed, and just two days later, she confessed with pride that she had helped those men escape.

When was she executed, and how?

Answer: She was found guilty of treason and was executed by firing squad on October 12, 1915.

Who was the first recipient of the Medal of Honor for heroism as a POW?

Answer: The first recipient was an executive officer from a naval vessel that was captured after his ship sank. Edouard

Izac was captured and moved from two different POW camps while keeping the information he had learned on the submarine on his way to the POW camp to himself in the hope the information could help the Allies.

Edouard Izac had made several trans-Atlantic transport runs before a German U-boat sank his ship. How many trips had he made?

Answer: Izac had made four other voyages delivering supplies and troops to the western front.

How did Izac escape from the POW camp?

Answer: He waited for the right time, and under cover of darkness, he climbed a barb-wired fence and escaped into the forest surrounding the camp. He worked his way to the Rhine, surviving on raw fruits and vegetables. Once he arrived at the Rhine, he swam across to Switzerland and made his way to the Bureau of Navigation, which he reached on November 11, 1918, the day the war ended.

What other accomplishments did Izac go on to achieve?

Answer: Izac would end up representing California in the House of Representatives for California from 1937-1947. He was also a member of the House of Naval Affairs

Commission. He was part of this when it inspected the concentration camps in 1945.

What were the 14 points that U.S. President Woodrow Wilson laid out to Congress?

Answer: When Woodrow Wilson stood in front of the Congress, his plan was to lay out a vision of what the post-war global community would be like. His 14 points included no secret treaties and alliances. He felt that politics should be transparent. The speech also stated that the seas should be neutral territory as well as all countries should be able to have free trade. It called for a global reduction of arms by every nation. The points also stated that Belgium should be reinstituted as neutral and independent once again.

Along with the territorial ideas, he also said that the Alsace-Lorraine should be retired to France and that Italy's borders should be drawn. Continuing with the boundaries and territorial questions, he also felt that the Balkan nations should be given independence and that those that were still under Turkish rule should be granted freedom. He also thought that the Kingdom of Poland should be given country status and more land. Lastly, these 14 points were the foundations for the League of Nations.

Who were the big four at the Paris Peace Conference?

Answer: The big four were the leaders of the big four nations in charge of overseeing the peace conference. This included: Wilson from the U.S., George from Britain, Clemenceau from France, and Orlando from Italy.

Historian

The war wasn't exactly a world affair. What country was neutral during the war?

Answer: Norway was the only European country that remained neutral for the war. They even tried to do the same in the next world war, but the Third Reich had different plans and invaded them in 1940.

There were a lot of new things to warfare during this war. Other than trench warfare, what two other military weapons also saw their first action during the conflict?

Answer: The two pieces of equipment that would wreak havoc on the battlefields of World War I were the tank and the flame thrower. The British introduced the tank at the Battle of Somme. The flame thrower was a weapon produced by the Germans.

Over nine million soldiers died during the war. A good majority of these were under 30. Some were even younger. How old was the youngest soldier to see action?

Answer: Many young men rushed to their enlistment stations and lied about their ages to join. The youngest was a 12-year-old British boy. Sidney Lewis would put boots to ground for the first time at the Battle of Somme in 1916. Eventually, his mom would produce his birth certificate, and he would be recalled. He would later re-enlist in 1918 and spend time in Austria as part of the army of occupation.

Trench warfare was new to war and used very effectively on both sides of the western front. Because it worked so well, quite a lot of trenches were dug. How many miles of trenches were there by the end of the war?

Answer: Throughout the war, the soldiers of both the Central Powers and the Allied Forces dug 15,659 trenches. (That was almost 16,000 miles of trenches along the western front.)

One of the most critical military strategies apart from trench warfare was maneuver warfare. What is the definition of maneuver warfare?

Answer: This battle strategy was a very effective form of tactic and resulted in many victories. The basic principle of this strategy is tactics infuse the enemy through disrupting their maneuvers with rapid movement. These swift attacks and actions kept the enemy on their toes, and this increases the chance that they make a mistake.

Another form of warfare strategy was known as attrition warfare. What does this strategy entail?

Answer: This type of warfare entails wearing down the enemy through the use of tactics like blockades as well as constant bombardment. The intention, when using this style of combat, is to wear your opponent down both physically and emotionally until their will is broken and they can no longer fight. During WWI, this type of warfare happened between 1915-1917.

You have to have the support of the people, and the Prussian Prime Minister knew this. What did Otto von Bismarck use to convince German people in the south to support the war efforts?

Answer: Just 40 years before the outbreak of WWI, the Prussian empire locked horns with France. This is the war that brought a unified Germany and granted Germany control over the Alsace Lorraine. Using a new German pride and the threat of them losing land, he was able to garner support.

The Treaty of Versailles was vital in the revolution of the war, but one country rejected the treaty. Which country was this?

Answer: The United States opted to reject the treaty on the grounds that they wanted to stay out of European political affairs.

Though the war ended for everyone with the Treaty of Versailles, the Russians left the battle well before the armistice, and the famous treaty. What was the treaty that allowed Russia to end its war with Germany?

Answer: Lenin's decision to pull out of the war came to fruition with the signing of the Treaty of Brest-Litovsk on March 3, 1918. The name of the treaty came from the city it was signed in, which is what we know today as Belarus. With the signing of this treaty, Russia ceded to giving up over a million square miles of land. Germany and the Austro-Hungarian Empire would gain control over Lithuania, Poland, Latvia, and Estonia. The Ottoman Empire would gain Kars, Ardahan, and Batum. Whereas Ukraine, Georgia, and Finland would gain independence. Of course, when Germany lost, they were forced to give up the land they had accrued with this treaty.

The Second Battle of Ypres happened in 1915 in Belgium. The battle lasted a little over a month and was the site of two significant firsts. What were they?

Answer: The Second Battle of Ypres would see the first use of Canadian troops as well as the first use of gas by the Germans. The Germans would effectively use chlorine gas as a weapon to help them win the battle. The gas would be a vital tool for the Germans, and immediately after this attack, the Allied Forces began working on their gas. The Canadian First Division served at Ypres and lost significant casualties. This battle would also give a brave Canadian the honor of being the first member of the Canadian Army to win a Victoria Cross.

Airplanes were new to battle and needed a few adjustments to make them useful. One of these improvements was a unique propeller. What was this propeller called?

Answer: The propeller was called the "Systeme Morane." This propeller was designed with triangular wedges made out of steel and included to stop bullets from striking the propeller.

How big was the eastern front?

Answer: The eastern front encompassed 310 miles of land and stretched from Memel (which was in East Prussia but is now part of Lithuania) on the Baltic Sea to Czernowitz on the Romanian border.

How large was the Russian Army when the war began?

Answer: At the beginning of the conflict, the Russian Army held steady at one million soldiers. By the end of the war, the army had risen to over three million.

The Germans had the Schlieffen Plan, what was the Russian plan of attack called?

Answer: The Russians developed a plan of attack that would have them splitting their forces. In the north, the Russian Army would take two of its divisions and attack east Prussia, while three armies would strike Austria-Hungary. This plan was called Schedule 19.

The *Lusitania* may be the most famous passenger ship sunk by German U-boats, but it was not the first. What was the first passenger ship to be sunk?

Answer: On March 11, 1915, the German U-boat, *U-28*, sunk the British passenger ship *RMS Falaba*. The ship left Liverpool bound for the western African coast. Off the smalls of the St. George Channel, the German U-boat attacked and fired on the boat.

The war spread across the globe, even onto U.S. soil. A group of German sympathizers attacked a factory, blowing it up in Jersey City. What did the factory make?

Answer: To help their comrades across the Atlantic, a group of German sympathizers snuck in and planted bombs in the Black Tom Island Munitions Plant on July 30, 1916. This plant was making weapons and ammunition for U.S. troops that had just recently entered the war effort. They hoped to stop the flow of supplies to the Allied Forces. In the explosion, four people were confirmed dead, but that number may be up to seven.

The war ended with an armistice, not an actual surrender. There were two separate treaties, one for each front. When did each central power sign their armistices?

Answer: After the fall at Trieste, the Austro-Hungarian Empire signed the Armistice of Villa Giusti. This treaty was signed on November 3, 1918. On the western front, the armistice was signed on November 11, after the Battle of Redonthes at Le Francport.

What is another name for the Battle of Jutland?

Answer: The major naval battle is also known as the Battle of Skagerrak.

Who was the chief of the general staff and principal strategist for the German forces at Verdun?

Answer: Erich von Falkenhayn was a Prussian general of some note before he took charge of the forces at Verdun. He gained experience training the Chinese soldiers that would fight against the boxers in the rebellion. He was promoted to the Prussian Minister of War before replacing General Helmuth von Moltke as the chief of the general of staff in 1914.

What was Falkenhayn's edict for the Battle of Verdun?

Answer: Falkenhayn went into the Battle of Verdun with strategy and goals. These goals seemed extreme to some as he wanted a five-to-one kill ratio and to take the citadel at Verdun at all costs. His was a war of attrition, and he didn't care how much French or German blood was needed to be spilled to achieve his ultimate goal.

What happened to Falkenhayn after the failure of the Verdun Offensive?

Answer: The failure of the Verdun campaign haunted Falkenhayn for the rest of his life. After the significant defeat and loss of soldiers, the German High Command decided he needed to be dismissed.

Where did (and still do) the bones of the fallen soldiers end up after the Battle of Verdun?

Answer: When the battle was over, the dead found a home at Douaumont Ossuary. To this day, bones discovered are taken to the ossuary and laid to rest with the rest of their comrades.

After the initial offensive, how much land was covered?

Answer: After the first battle of the Spring Offensive, the Germans had gained 1,197 square miles of land and had taken 90,000 prisoners.

What was the second wave during the Spring Offensive's code name?

Answer: The second wave of Spring Offensive was executed on April 9, 1918, and was less successful than the initial foray. This troop movement was dubbed Operation Georgette.

What did the Battle of Amiens and the subsequent battles become known as?

Answer: The Battle of Amiens was the opening battle of what would later become called the "Hundred Days" Offensive. This push would be the final nail in the German Army's coffin and lead to the armistice.

How many lines of trenches did the Germans have at the Battle of Amiens?

Answer: The German defensive line was fortified by a sequence of three lines of trenches. These trenches, however, were poorly crafted with inefficiently placed wire along with the top and poorly-built dugouts.

What was the "Amiens Gun"?

Answer: The "Amiens Gun" was a German 280mm Krupp naval gun mounted to a railway carriage.

How many infantry divisions were in Rawlinson's Fourth Army?

Answer: Once Rawlinson's Fourth Army was beefed up, there was a total of 14 different infantry divisions along with several cavalry and tank units.

How many pieces of artillery, tanks, and aircraft played a part in the Battle of Amiens on the side of the Allied Forces?

Answer: On the Allied side, the Battle of Amiens was stacked. Not only did they have 14 infantry divisions but also a total of over 2,000 artillery guns, over 600 tanks, and 1,900 plus several aircraft.

How many divisions, guns, and aircraft did the German Second Army have at the Battle of Amiens?

Answer: In the corner of the German defenses, the Second Army was stocked with ten divisions, 530 guns, and 365 planes.

What was a "Whippet" tank?

Answer: The Allied Forces had a tank dubbed the "Whippet" tank. This tank was a lighter, faster tank that the Allies used for scouting missions.

What Russian Army was annihilated at the Battle of Tannenberg?

Answer: As the battle came to a close, the Second Army was led by Aleksander Samsonov. With no help from his fellow generals, Samsonov's men were outmaneuvered and found themselves running to the cover of the forests, but it was too late; the defeat was imminent.

The defeat at Tannenberg was cemented by the tactics and strategies of the German leader of the opposition army, the Eighth Army. Who was this leader?

Answer: Paul von Hindenburg led the Eighth Army. Hindenburg had retired but was recalled to duty after the war began. He led the Eighth Army in conjunction with Erich Ludendorff, who sat in the position of chief of staff. Hindenburg would go on to become president of the Weimar Republic and was also the man who named Adolf Hitler as the German chancellor. In contrast, Ludendorff would end his military career in defeat and go on to serve in parliament.

How many Russians died during the Battle of Tannenberg?

Answer: The losses of the Russian Second Army were significant, which gave the Central Powers a boost of confidence going into the following months. Fifty thousand men were killed or injured, and almost 100,000 men were taken as prisoners.

What happened to the leader of the Russian forces?

Answer: This type of defeat was not acceptable to Samsonov, the general in charge of this arm of the attack, so early on the morning of August 30, he walked unnoticed into the forest and ended his life.

Many battles in this war and others are known by different names. What is another name for the Battle of Tannenberg?

Answer: Because it took place near a town called Allenstein, it is also known as the Battle of Allenstein.

What was the date that the pivotal Battle of Tannenberg began?

Answer: The opening salvos of the battle began on August 26, and the battle waged for four long days before coming to an end on August 30. It was one of the very first and most famous battles of the first year of war and set the tone for quite a while to come.

After the war, the boundaries of countries were redrawn. If you wanted to visit Tannenberg today, where would it be located?

Answer: Tannenberg is no longer called Tannenberg. Today you would find this city on the map by looking for Stębark, Poland.

What advantages did Lieutenant Colonel Max Hoffman have that helped the German forces defeat the Russians at the Battle of Tannenberg?

Answer: Hoffman knew the Russian politicals amongst the generals. He obtained this information after Schlieffen sent him to observe the Russians during the Russo-Japanese war. Here, he learned that the two Russian generals executing the movements in this area, Rennenkampf and Samsonov, did not share the same views nor like each other. This dislike would leave communication, for which the Russian Army was known to be careless with anyway, few and far between.

Who was the general in charge of the XX Corps who fought against Samsonov?

Answer: General Friedrich von Schulz led the 20th Army Division of the Eighth Army at the Battle of Tannenberg. He would later become the commander of the Eighth Army when it moved east to fortify the lines at the Battle of Verdun.

Where was Samsonov's Second Army based out of?

Answer: The Second Russian Army had to march from their stationed base in Warsaw.

What limited General Rennenkampf's ability to advance and carry out his part of the Battle of Tannenberg?

Answer: Several factors hampered his troop's advancement. With the fortifications of Konigsberg and the Masurian Lakes, which made communication with Samsonov practically impossible, he only had a small 40-mile gap to move his troops through.

The Turkish forces needed help with their organization and asked for help from their ally, Germany. Who was the German general that helped lead the Turkish forces?

Answer: After being asked for help, the Kaiser could see no one better for the job of reorganizing the Turkish forces in Constantinople than Otto Liman von Sanders. The Russians saw this move as a threat and soon realized that they were right as the Turkish began to move in to help the Balkans and the Caucuses.

What was the first battle of the Brusilov Offensive?

Answer: The Brusilov Offensive would end up being a very successful campaign for the Russian forces. The campaign would begin on June 4, 1916, with the Battle of Lutsk.

What did the French ask their allies to do in February of 1916?

Answer: The French wanted to weaken the German forces, so they reached out to both the British and the Russians to ask them to plan significant attacks at different points. They believed this would split up the German forces and help them gain some ground. Both parties agreed, with the British beginning the planning of the Battle of Somme and the Russians looking to attack both Lake Narocz and Vilna.

What did General Brusilov push for?

Answer: Brusilov was a strategist, and knowing that the attack of Vilna was planned, he knew a way to ensure the defeat of the enemy soldiers. He reached out to the Russian command and pleaded with them to allow him to move his troops to attack in the southwest. He knew this would cause the enemy troops to be split up and, therefore, weaken the Vilna line allowing for victory.

The north may have been a campaign against the Germans on the eastern front, but in the south, it was all about the Austro-Hungarian forces. Who led these forces at the Battle of Lutsk?

Answer: The heir to the Habsburg throne, Archduke Joseph Ferdinand, led 200,000 men against Brusilov.

The forces that marched against the Hapsburg Prince numbered how many?

Answer: Brusilov was outmatched when it came to numbers as he only marched with 150,000. This difference would mean he had to be more strategic and use his years of experience, which is what he did and why the Offensive was so successful.

How long was the front that Brusilov wanted to attack?

Answer: Brusilov felt that if he were able to attack a line that went from the Pripet Marshes to Bucovina, he would be able to draw enough troops from the other front that it would give his comrades up north a good-sized advantage. That led him to attack a 200-mile front with just 2,000 guns. Along his push, he would capture over 20,000 prisoners before the Offensive came to a close.

After the first two days of the Offensive, how many casualties were there?

Answer: The battle was fierce for the first two days and left the field and field hospitals with approximately 130,000 casualties.

The success of the Brusilov Offensive led to what two events elsewhere in the war?

Answer: Because of the loss of forces by the Austro-Hungarian Army, the offensive on the Italian city of Trieste by General Franz Conrad von Hötzendorf had to be ceased so he could send reinforcements to the line. There were also four divisions of the German Army relocated from the front lines of the Battle of Verdun to reinforce the Austro-Hungarian forces further. The loss of this division can be directly linked to the German's defeat at Verdun.

When did the Brusilov Offensive end?

Answer: The offensive lost steam and officially came to an end on September 20, 1916. After pushing his way along that 200-mile front, Brusilov and the Russian forces gained 9,650 square miles of territory and cost their adversary quite a few soldiers.

How did Brusilov train his troops for the upcoming offensive?

Answer: The first and most important aspect of the plan was total secrecy. Except for Brusilov and his troops, no one knew what the plan was. Along with this, Brusilov used life-sized replicas of the places he planned on attacking. Starting with artillery, he made sure that the sighting of these guns was seen by air reconnaissance.

What was the Central Powers' objective at the Battle of Mărășești?

Answer: The Romanian forces had been causing some trouble, and to take Romania, they knew they had to defeat the forces. The plan was for the German Ninth Army and the Austro-Hungarian First Army to encircle the Romanian Second Army and wipe them out.

Who were the opposing forces at the Battle of Mărășești?

Answer: On one side, you had the Romanians and the Russians. The Russians had begun to feel the weight of events back home and would eventually leave the Romanians to fight. The other side of the line was a combination of troops from Germany and the Austro-Hungarian Empire.

Each side had many generals leading their respective armies and divisions. Who were the commanders on each side?

Answer: On the Central Powers side, the big names leading the two armies were August von Mackensen and Karl von Wenninger.

On the Romanian front, the two significant leaders were Alexandru Averescu and Eremia Grigorescu. Dmitry Shcherbachev led the Russian forces.

The battle was intense, and though the Romanians were outgunned, they still held the advancing enemy off. How many troops, guns, and heavy guns did each side have?

Answer: The Romanians started the battle with just over 200,000 soldiers, 280 guns, and 36 heavy guns. On the other side of the front, the Central Powers rolled in with almost 250,000 soldiers, 223 guns, and 122 heavy guns. Along with that, the Central Powers also brought with them 1,135 heavy machine guns, two armored vehicles, and 365 mortars.

How many troops were lost on both sides during the Battle of Mărășești?

Answer: Even though the Central Powers had the advantage militarily, the Romanians knew the land and used this for their benefit. Because of this, the Romanians had fewer casualties when the smoke cleared. They only lost 27,410 soldiers in comparison to the 47,000 on the other side.

What strongholds and cities did the Allied Forces take after the Battle of Sharon?

Answer: By the end, the Ottomans had lost Afulah, Beisan, and Jenin as well as the cities of Nazareth, Haifa, and Samakh.

What was the unit called that was a mixed division that captured the Jordan River crossing in the Battle of Nablus?

Answer: The unit was a division comprised of both infantry and mounted cavalry. The force was named after its commander Edward Chaytor and became known as Chaytor's Force.

What type of unit was Richthofen assigned to after graduating from military school?

Answer: Though he became known for his aerial superiority, he started his illustrious military career with the First Uhlan Cavalry Unit.

Why did Richthofen request reassignment to an air unit?

Answer: He had success in his cavalry unit at the beginning of the war, even winning an Iron Cross for his service. This unit had moved from the eastern front to the western front, where they were used for supply delivery. Feeling that this was not prestigious enough for him, he looked for a change.

What was the first flying squadron he was assigned to, and who commanded it?

Answer: Planes were new to war, and there was not a lot of units, but Richthofen found his way into one of the flying squadrons. His reassignment was to the Jasta 2, under the leadership of Oswald Boelcke.

What type of plane was the iconic Red Baron best known for flying?

Answer: The first plane he painted red and flew into battle was the Albatross D.111, but toward the end of the war, he upgraded to the Fokker Dr.1.

When the Baron crashed and died, he was behind enemy lines. What happened to his body?

Answer: Allied troops recovered his body. Knowing who this was and his service to his country, he was laid to rest with full military honors.

Like with so many things, this iconic aerial ace was not only known by his famous moniker. What other names was the "Red Baron" known as?

Answer: Richthofen was also known as le Petit Rouge, the Red Battle Flier, or the Red Knight.

What was the name of the school Edith Cavell helped find?

Answer: She left England and made a name for herself teaching nurses in Belgium and eventually helped open the Berkendael Institute.

What two countries fought for a reprieve for Cavell?

Answer: Both countries that fought for the commuting of her sentence were both neutral at the time, but they felt that the punishment was harsh, seeing as she was a medical professional. The two countries that fought for her were the U.S. and Spain.

Where is there a statue to commemorate Cavell's bravery?

Answer: There is a statue in her home country of England in London. The statue is located in St. Martin's Place.

What village was Aníbal Milhais' unit stationed in?

Answer: His Portuguese infantry unit was stationed in the city of La Couture.

What was the German name for the battle that Aníbal made his heroic stand?

Answer: It was one of the pushes during the Spring Offensive. This stage of the attack was dubbed Operation Georgette.

For his bravery, what medals did Aníbal earn?

Answer: He earned a medal from not only Portugal but also France. From his mother country, he received the Ordem Militar da Torre e Espada. From the French, he was also awarded the Légion d'honneur.

When did Aníbal Milhais die?

Answer: The Machin Gun Milhais lived to the ripe old age of 74, passing in 1970.

What profession was Ecaterina Teodoroiu studying before the war broke out?

Answer: Ecaterina had been studying at a girl's school in Bucharest to become a teacher before the war began, and then she volunteered to fight for her country.

What made Ecaterina decide to ask for a transfer from being a nurse to fighting on the front line?

Answer: There were two main factors in her decision. As she treated the men that made their way back to the hospital, she was a nurse and was inspired by their patriotism. Then her brother was killed in action, and she felt she needed to avenge his death.

What rank did Ecaterina end her career as?

Answer: She ended up leading a 25-man platoon as a Second Lieutenant.

Where did Ecaterina die?

Answer: Ecaterina fought at the Battle of Mărășești. During the battle, she was shot in the chest or head, the stories conflict. But it is said, however, her last words were, "Forward men, I'm still with you."

What was the name of another ocean liner sunk by a German U-boat not long after the *Lusitania*?

Answer: The *Lusitania* was one strike, but once the *SS Arabic* was sunk as well and the Zimmermann Telegram was intercepted, the U.S. was in a position where there was no other choice but to throw their support behind the Allied Forces of the French and British.

How many tons of war munitions was the *Lusitania* carrying when it went down?

Answer: Though at first, there was a denial of any munitions on board, eventually, it was exposed that the *Lusitania* carried approximately 173 tons of war munitions and supplies.

What pope suggested a temporary stay of combat to allow the troops to celebrate Christmas in 1914?

Answer: On December 7, 1914, Pope Benedict XV stated that he felt it would be a sign of good nature of the men to lay down arms to celebrate the birth of the Lord. It was not received well by the higher-ups of either side.

Which side initiated the Christmas Truce of 1914?

Answer: The night before Christmas, carols floated over the land known as No Man's Land, and in the early hours of Christmas Day, the Allied troops heard the faint tiding of Merry Christmas. The Germans crossed No Man's Land without weapons to start a day of celebration.

What were some of the things exchanged between the soldiers as gifts?

Answer: There wasn't much to gift, but the soldiers used their ingenuity and gifted each other things like cigarettes and plum pudding.

What other more somber activity did some soldiers do during the truce?

Answer: Many fallen brethren's bodies had been stuck in No Man's Land that were unable to retrieve normally. So, to ensure their brothers had their way of having an honorable burial, some soldiers took this time to recover those bodies.

Why did the Japanese enter the war on the side of the Allied Forces?

Answer: Not only did they have an agreement with the British from 1902, but they wanted to begin expanding their power in the far east. This move was challenging to do with a German presence in China. So, they joined the Allied Forces to help but also to gain help in their expansion as well.

Why was the entrance of Japan into the war so pivotal?

Answer: Like the Germans, the Russians were faced with having to defend themselves on two fronts as the Germans had soldiers in Tsingtao in China. By Japan entering the war, not only were the Germans neutralized, but also having an ally on their eastern borders was helpful.

How many Zeppelin attacks in total were there on Britain?

Answer: There were fifty plus attacks executed on the nation of England.

What type of unit did Churchill serve in after he resigned his cabinet position in 1916?

Answer: Churchill picked up a gun and headed to the front to serve with the Royal Scots Fusiliers in France.

How much money was Germany tasked with reparations? When did they make the last payment?

Answer: The Germans were found to be the sole aggressor and were charged with paying reparations for the damages caused by the war. The bill came to 132 billion Reichsmarks or 33 billion U.S. Dollars. This large sum took decades to repay, and the final reparations for WWI were paid in September of 2010.

World War 2

Fascinating Second World War Stories Plus 200+ Trivia Questions for Your Trivia Domination

Introduction

The Great War had left Europe unsettled and the German people and government in turmoil. With devasting destruction and loss of life, the communities across the continent were fearful and perhaps more divided than ever. They lived in constant fear that this could happen again, and unfortunately, a little over 20 years later, it would, but on a grander and more devasting stage.

The players would be the same, but the carnage and utter disregard for human decency were on a whole new level. With a rise in nationalism and a madman at the helm of the German state, a series of invasions would ignite a conflict that lasted six long years and lead to over 30 countries sending their troops into a global battle the world had never seen. This war would leave lasting effects on the citizens of the world and birth some of the most atrocious events known to man. By the time the six years ended, approximately 60 million were dead, and six million of those were of the Jewish faith.

World War II was ignited long before the annexation of Czechoslovakia and Austria or the invasion of Poland. In fact, the largest spark came from the sanctions and restrictions put on the German state at the end of WWI. Allied forces and the nations that had been impacted by the aggression of both Germany and the Austro-Hungarian Empire feared that if the ramifications were not harsh enough, it wouldn't be long before the world felt the clutches of war once again.

Enter the Treaty of Versailles, which was signed on June 28th, 1919, and within its pages, the embers that would ignite the fire of the second great war could be found. The treaty made it painfully clear that Germany was the instigator of the war, and for this, they would pay greatly.

Along with a massive loss of land, which left seven million Germans now citizens of other countries, the Germans were fined an excessive amount of money—132 billion Reichsmarks. The treaty also took industry away from the German people and limited their military to just 100 thousand men.

Many proud German citizens felt humiliated by the laws of this treaty, and a rise in nationalism began to swell. The Nazi Party and its leader, Hitler, would use the ramification of these clauses to gain a foothold and eventually full power of the German Republic.

The German economy was hit the hardest by the Treaty, and as the economy took a turn and hyperinflation took hold, nationalism became exacerbated. In 1923-1924, Germany experienced hyperinflation the world has never seen as prices skyrocketed, and even bread—which at one point cost a billion Marks—was too expensive for the struggling German populace to afford. The unemployment rate increased exponentially due to the loss of control of their industrial sector. That, coupled with the inflation of prices, left many Germans struggling to eat and take care of their family. The rising of prices for everyday goods agitated the ire of the populace and left them open to the idealistic platforms of the newly-formed German Workers' Party—which would become the Nazi Party.

If the economy continued in this way, the German leaders would never be able to make their reparations, and so the Dawes Committee was formed. This Committee met in January of 1924, in the hopes that they could solve Germany's problems. The way to get this done was by balancing budgets and stabilizing the German currency. By the time the report came out in April, it was clear that both sides were in favor. With a restructuring of the German Reichsbank and a loan of 800 million Marks to Germany from the U.S., the problem was solved. These two points would bring a boon to the German economy throughout the rest of the roaring '20s.

Everything ran smoothly until October of 1929. Thanks to the expansion of the U.S. stock market, there was some imbalance and undue stress on the financial world. The signs of a crash had already begun, and with low wages, excessive debt, and outstanding loans, the stock market plummeted. In order to shore up the dam, all American investors began recalling loans, even the ones to governments like the one to Germany. Unable to pay it, the German economy plunged along with a good chunk of the world into an economic depression.

All of this shined a giant spotlight on the inefficiency of the Weimar Republic Government. Their inability to create jobs and manage their economic turmoil became evident. The poorly-run government allowed the wave of extremism and nationalism to continue to build within Germany. Taking advantage of this ill-functioning government, the German socialists saw an opening and began organizing for a revolution that would take over a decade to come to fruition.

Chapter One
Rise of The Third Reich

The moment the pen hit the paper and the ink was dry on the Treaty of Versailles, the weight of the excessive sanctions began to take its toll on the German economy and people. The elite of German society, dissatisfied with the interim government and the subsequent Weimar Republic, started to gather in beer halls and backrooms in an effort to rile the German people up and invigorate them to save Germany and bring back its honor.

One of these individuals was Dietrich Eckart, who was a well-known playwright and journalist. He, along with other members of his political circle, had been looking for a confident and charismatic individual to lead the German Workers' Party since its inception in 1919. Little did Eckart know that the German military was going to send him the perfect candidate.

In September of 1919, the German military was hearing more and more about extremist meetings taking place in several of the Munich beer halls. This kind of rhetoric would never do. These extremists were spewing anti-republic statements and socialist points of view aimed at undermining the Weimar Republic. In order to get a handle on these radicals that seemed to be gaining steam with the German people, the military intelligence division began inserting spies into the proceedings.

One of these was a young man named Adolf Hitler. As young Adolf sat and listened to what the party leaders were saying, he found himself agreeing with them and unable to complete his mission. Then one night in a fever of excitement, Adolf set his notepad down, stood up from the table, and began to speak.

The party leader, Anton Drexler, and Dietrich Eckart, Drexler's right hand, watched on. Eckart was mesmerized and soon realized he had found what he had been looking for in this disheveled but passionate young man. Drexler, though, wasn't convinced, but Eckart's excitement about this boy's future pushed the idea anyway. Soon, Adolf was not only a member of the German Workers' Party but a vital tool used to spout its propaganda and the party's 25-point plan to elevate and transform Germany back to its former glory.

Hitler rose through the ranks of the party quickly, and by July of 1921, he became the head of the party, removing Anton Drexler as the party leader. Along with this new leader came new ideas, and the first thing would be a new name. Hitler, encouraged by his new place in the hierarchy, would urge his comrades to adopt the name National Socialist German Workers' Party (NSDAP), and this version of the GWP would become the Nazi Party that would lead Germany into a war with the rest of the world.

Europe was changing, and with that change came a surge of nationalism and socialism—why shouldn't Germany be riding the wave? For instance, in Italy, Benito Mussolini had seen an opening and seized power. Hitler was intrigued by the way Benito Mussolini had used division and Italian nationalism to work his way into power. (Later, in Hitler's push for European dominance, Mussolini would become an ally).

Hitler would encourage his party to follow suit and attempt a coup. The party would have to start small, and why not in their very own corner of Germany, Bavaria. Then once they had a hold of the government in Bavaria, they could turn their attention to the capital, Berlin. There had been rumblings of the leaders of Bavaria talking of a fight for independence. Hitler and his inner circle knew if they were going to make their move, it would have to be soon.

However, though Hitler had been leading the party well, the inner circle of the party wasn't sure the old guard politicians of the Bavarian province would be convinced by this upstart. They sought support from a German war hero, Erich Ludendorff. Once Ludendorff had signed on, the plan was formulated.

On the night of November 9th, 1921, the Nazi Party would march on one of the Munich beer halls where the leaders of the city were allegedly meeting to discuss Bavarian succession from the German state. Along with this location, the plan was to take control of other key sites, like the police station, to ensure the turnover of power went without a hitch.

The Nazi SA brownshirts and Hitler himself would take the beer hall while more brownshirts and their leader, Ernst Rohm, would concentrate on the police station. Once Hitler had secured the beer hall, Ludendorff would arrive and appeal to the German politicians on behalf of the party.

The plan was sound and may have worked if all had happened as discussed. Hitler railed at the captured Munich leaders, insisting they relinquish control, and that there needed to be a change in Germany for the state to gain its once former glory. It seemed as if they would all stick to their convictions even after Hitler, in a fit of rage, pointed a gun at one of their heads. The wheels were coming off this plan, and someone desperately needed to get them back on.

The one tool the party had that could sway these stubborn elitists was Ludendorff, and unfortunately, he was running late. Ludendorff finally arrived, and seeing that Hitler was clearly struggling to convince his comrades to join the cause, he took over the negotiations. Tired of dealing with the high and mighty politicians, Hitler left to address other issues that had arisen while Ludendorff pleaded with the captured leaders to change their minds. Seeing that it was going to take more effort to get the politicians on the side of the party, Hitler ordered the rest of the missions scrapped for now. The party still had one big move up their sleeve, but first, Ludendorff would have to do the job he was hired to do.

Ludendorff would appeal to the captured leaders' German pride and better judgment. After all was said, one of the men would stand up, shake hands, and agree to stand on the side of Hitler and the Nazi Party. However, this was a lie, and he never intended to back Hitler's play for power. The moment they were free, he planned to take down this right-wing extremist group and free Germany from their insane ideology.

The following morning, Hitler and Ludendorff, along with members of the Nazi Party, gathered once again and, with conviction, marched to the center of town, intent on claiming their vestry and announcing they were now in power. Unfortunately for Hitler and his cronies, that was not what happened. The three thousand plus Nazis that marched were met with a volley of fire from the Munich police. Mayhem ensued, and several Nazis were killed or injured, including Hermann Goring—this would send him into the arms of an addiction that would plague the rest of his life. Hitler escaped. After two days of searching the city from top to bottom, the Munich police finally found and arrested Hitler.

After Hitler and several of his inner circle, including Rudolph Hess and Ernst Rohm, were imprisoned, the Bavarian state looked to make an example of them. The only way to show the people they were not going to take this was a very public trial. Making this a public spectacle would mean inviting the media to be part of the proceedings, and once this was done and the stage set, the trial pushed on.

Hitler saw the media as a way to get his name and message out to the whole of Germany. Seizing the free press, Hitler prepared to go off on tirades that would be nothing more than his beer hall speech. These tirades were effective, though. Not only was this right-wing extremist now known throughout Germany, but he had been able to sway many of the very people that had put him here—there was validity in what he was saying.

Many historians feel that was why when all was said and done, Hitler was given a mere five-month sentence.

Though the verdict was more like a vacation as he was given not only a personal assistant—Rudolf Hess—but also anything he asked for. His cell was littered with books, a gramophone, and looked more like an office than a prison cell. Hitler was even allowed guests and continued working with the party throughout his sentence.

As Hitler and his assistant wiled away their time, Hess began to stroke Hitler's ego, raving about his leader's genius. Eventually, at the behest of Hess, Hitler would begin to jot down his thoughts and ideas, and when he was released in December of 1924, he had the beginning of his famous but vitriolic novel "Mein Kampf." The final manuscript would not be finished until the middle of 1925. With the publishing of this book, the personal ideologies of Hitler were laid out in great detail. Many of these ideas would form the base for the horrific and evil machinations of the Third Reich.

While Hitler had been in prison, the party had begun to rebuild and started to turn away from much of the ideology of pre-beer hall putsch Nazis. Even with this pivot from the party's initial platform, Hitler would soon find his footing within the party once again and steer it toward a less bloody form of a coup.

When Hitler emerged from his cell, he knew where the party had gone wrong. The use of force and violence would not work in this country as it did in Italy. Instead, the Nazis' way into power would be to take control of the political institution. Over the next several years, Hitler and his Nazi Party would begin working their way into the Reichstag. Their views, however, were still hard to get the German people to back, as the country was riding a wave of prosperity. But fate would soon bring them the misfortune they needed to gain the attention of the German people.

In 1924, the Dawes Plan was enacted, which tied Germany's economy directly to the economy of the U.S., and in 1929, when the stock market crashed, so did Germany's economy. Over the next several years, the Nazi Party would work their way to a majority rule in the Reichstag. They would also find ways to introduce censorship as well as remove the German people's civil liberties.

By July of 1933, Hitler had passed the Enabling Act, making him a dictator for four years and allowed for the dissolution of all other political parties, leaving the Nazi Party the only legal political party left. Hitler's power was almost absolute except for the presence of President Hindenburg.

On August 2nd, 1934, that last obstacle was removed when the mighty WWI war hero, President Hindenburg, died. After this tragedy, amidst the mourning for the beloved leader, Hitler would merge the president and chancellor post and become the supreme leader of the German state. The Nazi plan could now be freely implemented, and there was no one to stop them!

1935-1939: WWII Begins

With the power firmly in Hitler and the Nazis' hands, they were free to begin putting their ultimate plan in motion. The scheme started in the spring of 1935, with the institution of their first assault on the Jewish community of Germany. Over the following months, the party would take away the right for German Jews to fly the flag, to serve in the military, and they outlined a way to define what it was to be Jewish, as well as stripped those they deemed Jewish of their German citizenship.

The culmination of these acts would lead to the Nuremberg Laws, which were the tool by which the atrocities of the Holocaust would be propagated. Amidst the flurry of anti-Jewish laws and decrees, Hitler also announced the reformation of the German military. The German industrial complex would start the race to rearmament—though this was already being done in secret—and building the German military into a machine that would unleash its wrath four years later.

If 1935 was the launch of their war on the Jewish population of Europe, then 1936 was the consolidation of power in regards to the police and control of the overall German populace. The state police would be merged and placed under the control of two of Hitler's inner circle, Hermann Goring and Henrich Himmler.

For the police forces in the Prussian province, they would report to Goring's Gestapo, while the remainder of Germany would fall under Himmler's Schutzstaffel, otherwise known as the SS. Hitler, and his leadership knew if they were going to control the narrative and bend the people to their will, they were going to need control of all military forces, and this included local police. Alliances would also play a part in 1936. The Reich needed to form partnerships with like-minded individuals as well as other empires that might throw a hitch in their expansionist plans.

Hitler started with his neighbor to the south and fascist dictator, Benito Mussolini. The Pact of Steel was an agreement initially meant to be with Italy and Japan but would eventually just be between the two European nations.

To solidify support when the war broke out, Hitler knew that having Mussolini on his side would be beneficial. Plus, Hitler respected and admired Mussolini for his leadership and control over his people. Japan would be left out of the actual signing of the treaty as they did not have the same focus as the two other nations. Japan, having had years of confrontation with the Russians, wanted to focus the conflict on that front, but Germany and Italy knew that Britain was far more dangerous.

Along with these treaties and agreements, Hitler also sided with Spain's fascist leader, Franco. It seemed like Hitler was quietly moving his pieces into place to begin his push back against the Allied forces that had forced Germany into signing the Treaty of Versailles. The first shot across the bow would be the re-entry into the Rhineland of German troops.

That same year in August, Hitler's new Reich would be under the scrutiny of the world as Berlin would be the stage for the Olympics. The months leading up to this event were filled with concealment of what had been occurring in Germany over the last two years. Hitler took money from the coffers to build new and exciting buildings to enforce the economic solvency and physical strength of the new German Reich.

The propaganda and atrocities committed against the Jewish citizens of Germany were wiped away and hidden. He wanted the world to know that they had not defeated the German people, that they were strong, proud, and ready to be a force in the world economic stage. Hitler wanted to make a statement and took significant measures to do so.

Under the world's watchful eyes, Hitler had managed to build the German Army up with no push back from Britain or France, and in January of 1937, he made his intentions very clear. Standing in front of the Reichstag, Hitler called for Germany to withdraw from the Treaty of Versailles. This decree would send ripples throughout Europe, and yet still, there was no retaliation or push back from the Allied forces. With his intentions out in the open just 11 months later, Hitler would gather his military leaders and plot out the plans for German expansion—or reclamation of German lands as he called it—and war.

The push would begin in the spring of 1938. Hitler's campaign to reunite all German-speaking people of Europe would commence with the annexation or Anschluss of his homeland, Austria. Word of the German's intention to take Austria found its way into the ear of the Austrian chancellor. Knowing he had only one chance, Chancellor Kurt von Schuschnigg immediately asked for a meeting with the Fuhrer. He hoped to keep Austria as an autonomous state, but this would not be the case. Instead, Hitler, using his power, urged the chancellor to appoint Nazis to his cabinet and call for a national vote on the Anschluss. The vote would not take place, though. The Austrian chancellor, under pressure from the Reich's leader, resigned from his post just two days after the meeting. The chancellor knew his nation would not stand a chance against the Nazi forces and so he stood before his people and pleaded for them to offer no resistance. The people listened, and on March 12th, German forces led by Hitler moved into the country, greeted by adoring throngs of Austrians. The next day, the annexation was made official, and Hitler had been successful in the first step of his plan.

Once Hitler rolled into Austria, the next target was the Sudetenland, which was part of Czechoslovakia. The Sudeten Germans had been helping the Nazis prepare this maneuver for quite a while. In 1919, with the Treaty of St. Germain, the strip of land that includes Bohemia and Moravia was given to Czechoslovakia. The native Germans that were left behind this new border felt as if they were disconnected from their heritage, and many felt persecuted by the native Czech population. When Germany and the Nazi Party began its rise, they initiated preparations for reunification with their motherland.

In the fall of 1938, it was time, and Hitler demanded that the German-speaking region of Czechoslovakia be returned to Germany. Its people were set free from the persecution they had been exposed to. Germany moved troops into the Sudetenland, and finally, the world took notice.

The Allied forces felt that Hitler had pushed the envelope just a little too far, and the leaders of Italy, France, and Britain joined Hitler in Munich—the Czech people were not represented in the meeting—to discuss Hitler's demands. In the end, the Treaty of Munich was signed. In this, it was decided that the land would be returned to Germany. The agreement was made with the understanding that the area in question was all Hitler and Germany wanted. With a peace treaty signed, the leaders returned home to their countries, looking like heroes. With the matter settled, Hitler's forces rolled into the Sudetenland, occupied in the spring of 1939.

While the German troops stood their ground in the Sudetenland, Hitler moved on to his next land grab. He felt there was another nation that had received quite a bit of land that was German by right, Poland. In January of 1939, Hitter declared that the city of Danzig to be German and proclaimed its people would soon be reunited with their brethren.

The statement ignited a flurry of anxiety in Britain and France. The two countries now feared that German aggression was all but a forgone conclusion. Not ready to begin his assault on Poland yet, Hitler turned his attention back to Czechoslovakia and marched deeper into the country, occupying its entirety and breaking the Treaty of Munich. Now with a sufficient foothold in Czechoslovakia, he could focus all his attention on Poland.

Worried that the Russians would attack his troops from the east if he pushed too far into Poland, Hitler and his military leaders decided that the only way to stop that was to enter into a treaty with Russia. Although Hitler was bitterly opposed to the idea of communism, he knew this was the only way to ensure that his efforts to push into Poland would be successful.

In August of 1938, Hitler and Stalin met and signed a non-aggression pact in which there was a detailed clause on how Poland would be divided between the two mighty empires. With that taken care of, Hitler was now free to send his troops into Poland, and that is precisely what he did.

With this blatant disregard for the laws laid out in the Treaty of Versailles, France and Britain now had no other choice but to declare war, and WWII began!

Chapter Two
1940: Expansion of The Axis Powers

The remaining months of 1939 would come to be known as the "phony war," as there were no military movements after Germany had taken Poland.

In 1940, that would change. There would be expansion by German forces into neighboring countries and an all-out assault on Britain. The Axis powers would solidify their alliance as Germany, Japan, and Italy would sign an agreement to help support each other militarily as well as economically.

Germany wouldn't be the only one of the Axis powers expanding; Japan and Italy would try their hand at it as well. On the Allied side, there were expansionist moves as the

Russians extended their power base into Eastern Europe and the Balkans. Hitler and his Nazi inner circle would also continue building on the foundation of hatred and open the concentration camp that would become synonymous with the Holocaust.

Invasions & Occupations

With the success of Poland, the Germans knew that their new battle strategy, known as "Blitzkrieg"—lightning war, may be the key to their success. The concept was not unique; in fact, the Germans had been sitting with this strategy in their back pocket since the late 1800s, only then it was called the concentration principle.

A 19th-century Prussian general had suggested the principle as a way to hit fast and hard and minimize casualties. General Carl von Clausewitz, in this principle, suggested that a concentrated blow against a specific target, when executed fast and furious, would limit the time it took to conquer the chosen target along with the decreased cost of munitions and lives.

The German military forces were now better-equipped thanks to the secretive rearmament that had occurred over the previous two decades. That, coupled with the Nazis' use of

Pervitin—a pill distributed to the German front line troops that was a form of methamphetamine—allowing the German Army to sweep into several nations quickly in the early months of 1940.

But before Hitler and the Reich would tear through the low countries and France, they had their eye set on controlling the North Sea and its access to the Atlantic. This objective meant moving into both Denmark and Norway. Denmark fell quickly as the king knew his army was not big enough or skilled enough to defeat the German military. Understanding this and not wanting excessive loss of life and property, the king surrendered with minimal push back.

The Norwegian front, on the other hand, would take a little work. The plan was set, the German Navy would move into several Norwegian ports on April 1st and take control in the water version of a Blitzkrieg. Unfortunately, they would meet some strategic problems and would end up not pushing into those ports for another eight days. With this opening, Britain rushed into the ports and waters surrounding them and lay mines to help protect neutral Norway and keep the Germans from getting access to open waters.

The Brits' plan was thwarted with care as German forces navigated their way safely through the minefields. It took more than training and excellence, though, to deliver the German victory. The Germans had an inside man, a commander that was loyal to Norway's former prime minister, Vidkun Quisling, a pro-fascist who made the landing possible.

This commander received word from the men above him that he and his soldiers were to fight with everything they had to stop the Germans from setting one foot on Norwegian soil. But the commander defied the order and instructed his troops to lay down arms when German forces landed. Once the Norwegian troops had fallen in several ports, the German minister in Oslo called on the leaders of Norway to surrender. But the Norwegian Government refused.

The German military leaders knew that Norway could potentially make this decision, and they planned according to a plot for the second wave of attack.

Over the skies of Norway, the sounds of German airplanes drifted through the air. As the Norwegian forces and citizens looked to the sky, hundreds of parachutes could be seen floating over the cities. The Germans decided if they couldn't land troops from the sea, they would take Norway from the skies. Using their air dominance, the German military secured their victory.

Once the Germans had taken control, they also realized they needed someone they could control in power, someone who shared their same ideology. For this job, Hitler chose to place the former prime minister, Quisling, in charge.

Even with the Germans assuming power over the central part of the Norwegian Government, there were Norwegian forces that refused to admit defeat. These forces, combined with help from the British, would continue to fight the German regime. The Norwegian resistance fought on, but once the British realized their allies to the south, the French, needed their help, they pulled out of Norway. The British removal of troops left the Norwegians no other choice but to admit defeat and begin years of subjugation by German rule and ideology.

In May of 1940, with the coastal regions of the North Sea well under their control, the Germans turned their eyes toward an old familiar enemy, the French. The Allied forces knew this would be their next move and moved to reinforce the area near central Belgium. After all, this was the path that they had taken in WWI, and it seemed only logical that they would repeat such a successful push.

However, this tactical decision would be a tragic miscalculation, as the German Wehrmacht, with their new strategy, blitzed through the southeastern area of Belgium and pushed their way through the Ardennes Forest and into Luxembourg. The new Panzer Divisions, backed by mobile infantry and artillery, were able to quickly rip through the forest and break through the Allied defensive line. Coupled with air support from the dominant Luftwaffe and superior radio communications, the German forces pushed hard and fast toward the English Channel.

With every step, German soldiers pushed the British Expeditionary Forces (BEF) to the coast, eventually stopping the drive at Dunkirk. The British felt the fury of the Reich and, having nowhere to push back to, were left with no other choice but to evacuate over 300,000 troops from the beaches near Dunkirk. The bay was shallow and the waters were choppy as soldiers began trying to leave the shores. The British troopships were unable to navigate their way in the waters and had to rely on French support.

This support didn't come from the military but from local merchants who had smaller ships that could pull close enough to the beach to load the British troops. The Germans had succeeded in pushing the British out of the area. However, they failed in the utter annihilation of their forces.

The victory in the north of France allowed the German Army to turn their attention to taking Paris and moving further into France.

For the next two months, Germany and France would be embroiled in vicious combat. In the end, though, the Germans would come out of the battle victorious. At the end of June 1940, after they had taken in Paris, the French sued for peace. Hitler agreed but wanted to make a statement and decided to move the train car that the Allied forces and German leadership had met in to begin discussions of an armistice in WWI.

The truce would cede northern France and the coastline to the German Reich and provide provisions that the new French Government would have to cooperate with Germany. This new French Government, also known as the Vichy Government, would be headed by WWI hero, Marshall Henri Petain. Soon after signing the armistice, Marshall Petain declared the new France neutral in Germany's war with Britain.

Romania and Hungary would also join the Axis powers in 1940. In June, the Russian forces moved into provinces of Romania—see Russian Expansion (p.40). The incursion of Russian troops into Romania caused the Romanian King, Carol, to reach out for help, and to keep the growing fascist parties on his side, he opted for an ally they could get behind, Germany.

Early in July, Romania became an ally with the Reich. This alliance would not be enough for the Reich, and eventually, Germany would invade and take absolute control of the country. Hitler did this to keep the Russian expansion from moving any further into Europe than it already had.

The other Axis powers also took their hand at invading and expanding their territory. Italy had been occupying Libya since before the First World War, which made a move to Egypt the next logical step. In fact, Mussolini had dreamed of expanding Italy back to the glory days of the Roman Empire, and that meant conquering Egypt. It didn't hurt that by doing this, he would also gain control over the Suez Canal, which could be a great benefit to the Axis powers' war efforts as well as build his strength in the Mediterranean. With the Battle of Britain underway, he felt the time was perfect and, in September of 1940, instructed his generals to begin their move.

The attack started on the cold evening of September 12th. An airdrop rained down bombs, and in the morning, this was followed by a massive barrage from artillery troops. With the path cleared, the forces from Libya crossed the Egyptian border. Over the next few days, the Italian forces made their way to Maarten-Mohammed, and this is where the invasion stalled. In the end, this invasion was an utter disaster, and the Italians had to admit defeat. Italy would also have a similar experience in Greece. With his forces already occupying neighboring Albania, Mussolini looked once again to conquer another land that was once part of the Roman Empire. Still, he was unprepared and had no tactical advantage, and this invasion failed as well.

Japan's efforts would be much more successful. At the beginning of the year, the Japanese leaders had been urging the French Colonial Government of Vietnam to allow them to land soldiers on their shores in order to continue their ongoing war with China. Until May, when Germany invaded France in the west, their request had fallen on deaf ears. After the French surrendered, the colonial government found themselves between a rock and a hard place and realized they would also have to sign an armistice with Japan.

It took months for everything to be ironed out, and in September, the first troops landed in Vietnam. Unhappy with the arrangement they had signed, the Japanese force switched to invading the country and, in just a week, seized complete control over the country. Over the next four years, the two powers would co-exist, much like the Vichy Government did with the Nazis in the west.

Russian Expansion

The Axis powers were not the only participant in the war that felt a desire to expand their influence and borders in 1940. After the Russians successfully gained ground in Poland, they knew that the Germans were not going to stop pressing east. Their only course of action would be to beat them to the punch and begin pushing into critical areas. In the summer of 1940, the Soviets sent an ultimatum to the Romanian Government: give up the territory of Bessarabia and Bukovina or face the might of the Soviet Army. The Russian leadership claimed that Bessarabia was already wholly Ukrainian, which was a Soviet state. As for

Bukovina, this annexation was reparation for all the damage done by Romanian rule in Bessarabia.

The following day, in a desperate move to stand up to the Russian invasion, the king of Romania gathered together his advisers as well as the Italian and German ambassadors. In this meeting, King Carol II made it clear he did not want to back down and that he would look to his allies for help in convincing Romania's neighbors Hungry and Bulgaria to help keep the Russian military from moving in. However, the two ambassadors offered him another suggestion, simply stand down and let the Russians take what they wanted.

The relinquishing of the land would save the bulk of Romania and appease the Russians. There was, of course, selfish interest backing this decision as the German ambassador knew that the Reich had plans to annex Romania at some point, but even still, it did seem like the only way to keep the Russians at bay. Not wanting to surrender so quickly, the Romanian ruler and several of his advocates debated back and forth. Eventually, a day later, they would err on the side of caution. After just two days after the first warning, the Romanian Government and the king agreed to cede the lands to the Soviets in hopes of keeping the peace.

In early June 1940, the Soviet Navy began the move to control the Baltic states of Lithuania, Estonia, and Latvia. The barricade started with a complete blockade of Estonia. The Russian Premiere, Vyacheslav Molotov, accused the Baltic states of conspiring against the Soviet Union and, as much as he would do with Romania, sent the three separate countries an ultimatum: surrender or have the Russian military complex invaded. All three countries did not have the forces to put up and fight, so they decided it would be best to allow the occupation of their lands.

Though there was some resistance in Estonia, it wasn't enough to keep the dominant Soviet Army from rolling in and seizing power. Along with the military invasion, the Russian leadership wanted to ensure their ideology was shared with their new subjects. A political coup was planned, and the Soviets placed "People's Governments" in power, each headed by one of Stalin's cronies or heads of the local communist party.

In mid-July, elections were held so these governments would be firmly under Soviet control in the Baltic states. This election was a farce, as only communists or supporters were allowed to run, and the Soviet candidates were announced as winners. The rest of the world would learn of this, but the communist propaganda machine would make it look like the Baltic nations had asked to join the Soviet Union.

Auschwitz Opens

In the years building up to the war, Germany had already begun to put the "Final Solution" in place. For those that opposed the Nazi ideology or regime, they would find themselves being arrested and placed in camps, which would later turn from prisons into tombs for a majority of those that entered through their gates. By the time the war had broken out, there were six of these camps up and running, and though they had not reached the pinnacle of cruelty and grotesqueness yet, they were still horrible places. The first camp was opened in 1933, outside of Munich. The Dachau concentration camp opened its gates and became the model for every camp to come.

That, of course, included the largest and most gruesome concentration camp of all, Auschwitz. With the outbreak of war and the annexation of Poland, the construction of Auschwitz's first camp was greenlit. The choice of where to build was a crucial decision—settling on a military base and its surrounding area. Auschwitz would be built outside of a small town in southern Poland, Oswiecim, near Krakow.

Auschwitz was initially designed to be another concentration camp for anyone who did not fit the idea of the perfect Aryan or enemies that the party felt could cause problems in the future. The commander in charge of the concentration camp and overseeing of its construction, Rudolf Höss, realized that the land of the military base would not be enough. His troops set out to confiscate factories as well as homes to make room for the camp. It took only a couple of months to have the camp up and running, and in the spring of 1940, the doors opened.

The Nazis needed a place to store their enemies and traitors to the cause, and its enormous complex was perfect. As SS leader Himmler, Hitler, and the rest of the Nazi Party put their final sinister plan in order, the purpose of Auschwitz would change immensely. No longer was it to be a mere concentration camp with the implementation of this plan; it would become an extermination camp.

The Nazi leaders looked for a place that would be the most logistically sound, and since Auschwitz was located in the center of the land the Reich had accumulated, it seemed like the perfect choice. Along with this location, the camp sat at the conjunction of approximately 40 different rail lines, which would make the transport of hundreds of thousands of Jews easier. Eventually, Auschwitz would be expanded to include Birkenau as well as 40 other smaller facilities, all with the express purpose of committing genocide.

British War Affairs

With the fall of France, Hitler's next big goal was to break his non-aggression treaty with Stalin and move on to Russia. But before he did this, he knew he needed to eliminate the British threat. So before he set out to take on the Red Army, a plan for Operation Sea Lion was drafted to neutralize the English and their military. Eventually, he planned on a full-scale invasion, but Hitler and his military leaders recognized the key to a successful troop landing would be to take out as much of the RAF as possible.

Hitler prayed that the reputation of his Luftwaffe would be enough to paralyze the British forces and lead to a quick and peaceful surrender. Sure that this would be the case, the Reich Fuhrer reached out with the offering of peace to the newly-appointed prime minister. Winston Churchill would have nothing to do with the treaty proposed. In fact, just days before the fall of France, Churchill stood before parliament and gave a rousing speech that praised the prowess of the RAF command and incited morale and patriotism throughout the great nation.

Churchill's speech dashed any hopes that Hitler had of peace with the British. Frustrated, the German leader and his generals reluctantly moved on with their plan. Both knew that logistically, the German forces were unprepared to take on this endeavor. Herman Goring alone felt that this undertaking was going to be a rousing success. He was confident that his Luftwaffe would be able to destroy the British Air Forces without a problem. Goring was full of pride and confidence as he strolled into the war room. Dressed in his usual ostentatious uniform laden with his medals, Goring leaned over the table and moved the models around as he detailed the plans for his fellow military leaders and Hitler.

The first wave of bombing runs would be targeted on the coastal regions, in particular the radar stations, ports, and other defense posts. With their communications and defenses down, the Luftwaffe could begin moving in on the land, followed shortly after with the land troops. Hitler was a little reluctant, but the passion that Goring showed as he bellowed out his strategy won him over, and he gave the go-ahead. On July 10th, 1940, Goring's Luftwaffe began their assault. For the next month, the German Air Force bombarded location after location, but the attacks were not nearly as effective as Goring had promised.

The raids on ports and other strategic points had had little impact on the capabilities of the British Air Force. Feeling that they required a more devastating tactic, word came down to the pilots of the Luftwaffe to begin moving inland to target airbases, RAF production sites, and the RAF planes as well.

The numbers were clearly in the Germans' favor, but the leader of the British Air Force, Chief Marshal Dowding, had a plan to combat that. He hoped this plan would drive the German troops back to defend their homeland. The British Air Force chose the perfect target, the German capital, Berlin.

On August 25th, 1940, the sound of British airplanes could be heard over the bustling streets of Berlin. Instead of targeting the city itself, the British leader chose a sight close enough to get Hitler's attention. The pilots had been ordered to target the Tempelhof airport. Dropping over 80 bombs on the capital, the British returned home hopeful that they had made a statement.

This act had done little damage to the city itself. The real damage done was to Hitler's pride, and in retaliation to this attack, Hitler and Goring began using the same tactic only to a more devastating extent. Moving their targets to the cities of England instead of military targets, the Blitz would be carried out in the dead of night to maximize the casualties, much like the Zeppelin raids of WWI. Looking to bring the Brits to the negotiation table, Hitler signed off on two large-scale raids on the capitol, London.

On September 15th, the first raid began. This tactic was an unfortunate decision as the Luftwaffe had been operating way beyond their means for quite a while. Along with overextending themselves, they were running short on supplies. Goring had begun to let the politics of the inner circle and this ego affect his leadership or decisions. This change left the Luftwaffe poorly led and utterly disorganized. The British were not sitting on their laurels either as they had introduced their new fighter plane. The Spitfire was one of the fastest aircraft in the world, and its maneuverability surpassed the German planes by leaps and bounds. The introduction of Spitfires led to the inability of the Germans to gain any kind of footing in British air space.

Seeing that this campaign was futile, Hitler retreated. All German pilots, in late October of 1940, were instructed to return home and begin preparing for other, more critical missions.

The Germans' miscalculation of British capabilities led to massive losses on both sides. But in the end, the British were able to overcome the numbers and stop the Germans from gaining control over their air space, and by doing this, stopped the inevitable German land invasion that was to follow.

This Battle of Britain was the first significant defeat for the Germans and served to show the rest of the Allies that the German war machine was not invincible.

Chapter Three
1941: Escalation of Hostilities

In 1941, the war would escalate, bringing more bloody battles to every corner of the globe. In the Pacific, the Japanese would invade further into mainland Asia as well as take several of the islands. These actions would cause the U.S. to set sanctions against them and drive a wedge further between the two nations. Eventually, that decision would lead to the first combat on American soil and push the U.S. into action.

The Italians would also expand their conquest and finally take Greece. However, their control would be short-lived, as the Germans would quickly stroll in and take the country for themselves. The Germans would also drive deeper into the Balkans, taking Yugoslavia and then turn to the east and set their sights on their ideological rival, Russia.

The Atlantic would see escalations of activity as well. Ships on both sides would be targeted and sunk.

Though the Germans had lost at the Battle of Britain, it was clear that they had the tactical advantage when it came to weapons and manpower. This strategic upper hand made Churchill nervous, and he knew he needed help from his ally across the Atlantic, the U.S. But the populace opinion of the American people was that they didn't want to get involved in another war that didn't affect them. This sentiment meant that Churchill's good friend Roosevelt would have to be clever in how he offered assistance. In March of 1941, the Lend-Lease Bill was passed, and the U.S. started production and delivery of supplies to the British and Allied forces.

Germans Break Their Pact

As Hitler began his plan in 1939 to take back the land from Poland that he felt was German by right, it was clear that he would have to step up his overtures to Stalin for a peaceful solution to the division of Poland. This realization would lead to the non-aggression pact, otherwise known as the Molotov-Ribbentrop Pact.

This pact was set to be valid for a decade and set out the division of influences for each nation in Eastern Europe. The terms of this treaty would suit the German leader as he began to annex the lands in Eastern Europe. However, in 1941, he was ready to set it aside and make a move on the Soviet Union and communism.

In the early morning hours of June 22nd, the Wehrmacht—German military—began its march eastward to the Soviet Union. With millions of men and thousands of tanks, the German Army marched with one goal in mind: expanding the Lebensraum.

Lebensraum was one of the ideologies Hitler used to explain his expansionist mindset. This concept stated that for the German people to develop naturally, they needed enough land. With this doctrine, it made sense that moving eastward was the best idea. The only thing in their way was the Slavic people and communism. Taking out the Soviet Union would kill two birds with one stone. The front to be covered started in the North Sea and ended at the Black Sea.

Like they did in the west, the German Army moved fast, and within the first month, drove their forces deep into Soviet territory, the panzers being the essential tool that made this campaign so effective. By the end of that month, German forces had surrounded both Minsk and Smolensk.

With these two significant cities all but taken, the rest of the armored troops raced toward the two gems of the Soviet Union, Leningrad—now St. Petersburg—and Moscow. However, with the German forces already more than halfway to their target, the campaign began to suffer from poor logistical execution and information. As the German Army drove deep, the Soviet forces did not give up quickly, and the counterattacks that they executed seemed to be extremely useful.

The success of these attacks stemmed from the soldiers knowing the land and the civilian allies that assisted them in their counterattacks. These movements stalled the German forces, which also began to suffer from a lack of supplies. In September, this lack of supplies was addressed with the arrival of new equipment and supplies. The appearance of these supplies allowed the Wehrmacht to move deeper into the Soviet Union and would lead to the blockade of both Kyiv and Bryansk-Vyazma.

The path to these cities was open, but the weather turned quickly, and heavy rains fell, turning the road into mud. The change in the weather halted the advancement of the German troops once again. But in November, the plummeting temperatures froze the fields and allowed the Germans to continue their drive. The harsh winter placed the Germans in a predicament as the Russian winters were not something that they were familiar with and ill-equipped to handle. But despite that, the commanders urged their men forward. The soldiers trudged through the snow and freezing temperatures finding their way both to Moscow and Leningrad.

At Leningrad, the Germans would lay siege to the city. This siege would last for the majority of the war (1941-1944), but confronted with severe counterattacks from the Soviet forces at the gates of Moscow, and the Germans had no other choice but to retreat. This push through the Russian countryside broke the pact, and it wasn't long until the Russians had jumped ship and joined the allied powers in their crusade against Hitler and the Third Reich.

Atlantic Conference

The U.S. had made it very known that they were staying out of the war, but Roosevelt and the government knew they had to lend some sort of support. Understanding this,

Roosevelt and Churchill would partner together, and soon the Lend-Lease Act was drafted.

The bill, on the surface, looked like another alliance, but among the lines of the document, there were direct objectives intended to allow the U.S. to play some role in the war to protect their investments.

In August of 1941, the two nations would meet to discuss what the world could be like post-war. For three days out of the prying eyes of the media and other countries, the two political titans sat aboard naval ships in the Placentia Bay—located in Newfoundland—and hammered out the eight points that were crucial to the future of the world. When all was said and done, the finalized document was released to the public on August 14th, 1941. It would be the document that helped the world rebalance itself after the terrors of this horrendous war.

In this document, the two countries agreed that there should be absolutely no territorial gains from the war. If there were land gains, they would only be allowed if the people of that territory agreed to it. This point in the contract was added to help keep any future expansionist regimes from gaining the amount of control the Third Reich had obtained.

Another feature of the Atlantic Conference was the proclamation that once the land was returned to people, they would be free to determine their government system.

The charter also had provisions regarding the economic impact of war and the idea of free trade. These concerns would be addressed by the concept of equal access to raw materials and no interference from outside nations when it came to signing trade agreements. The two men also agreed on another impact: global trade was the oceans. In this charter, international waters were discussed and had the principles laid out. Lastly, Churchill and Roosevelt dictated an idea of security within a state's borders and the disarmament of any aggressors.

Five months later, these ideas would be put in front of 26 governments, including the U.S., England, and the Soviet Union. It would become known as the Declaration by the United Nations and became the foundation for the United Nations. The signing of this declaration would ensure that the 26 countries that signed the document would abide by the principles outlined in its pages.

Attack on The United States

In the early morning hours of December 7th, 1941, the naval base at Pearl Harbor was just beginning to get its day started. Crewmen and soldiers were going about their daily lives, when out of the clouds above, a plane emerged, on its side, the rising sun of Japan. Following the dive bomber were 360 other planes, all bearing the same marking.

They began diving from the skies, unleashing bombs and sprays of bullets in what would go down as "a day that would live in infamy" for the United States. This vicious assault rocked the naval fleet and sent the U.S. barreling into WWII.

Even before the first bomb dropped on Pearl Harbor, the two nations, Japan and the U.S., were economic and political rivals. Japan looked to expand its influence in the east and to do that over several decades and instigated conflict with both Russia and China. Their interference in WWI also played a part in the U.S. sentiment toward the isolated island nation. Then in the '30s, when the depression hit the world, Japan looked to help its economy and push its expansionist agenda by invading China. The League of Nations would oppose this maneuver, and Japan would answer this condemnation by pulling out of the League.

Japan would then go on to commit several atrocities, including the Nanjing Massacre. The massacre was enough for the U.S., its government, and Roosevelt to do something. Since the United States was trying to keep from getting into wars, they used the only tools they had possible and began levying heavy embargoes on the Japanese. Along with restrictions on planes, oil, and metal, the U.S. also sent economic aid to the Chinese forces fighting off a Japanese invasion.

Then in September of 1940, Japan entered into a pact with Germany and Italy and became an official part of the Axis powers. Even with the signing of the Tripartite Pact, the U.S. continued to try to negotiate, but the Japanese kept expanding, taking several islands. The Japanese knew that war with the U.S. was inevitable, and they knew that the only way they could get the upper hand was to surprise the American fleet.

The target was clear; they would have to attack the fleet when the Americans weren't expecting it, and the perfect target would be Pearl Harbor. This battle plan seemed like a pipe dream to some of the Japanese leadership, but Admiral Isoroku Yamamoto knew that this would be their only chance of ensuring Japanese dominance in the Pacific. The logistical requirements of this fight were challenging. After all, the Japanese fleet would have to cover a lot of sea to get their planes close enough to do the job.

On November 26th, through the admiral, his fleet began their challenging trip. The fleet would run into a major storm that scattered their ships, but they were able to recover from that and keep cruising toward their final target. By the morning of December 4th, the fleet was able to make it their home base for their attack, which was just a few hundred miles north of Oahu. This position gave them the perfect strategic vantage point to launch their attack on Pearl Harbor.

The negotiations between the U.S. and Japan had begun to break down months before, and the U.S. Government and President Roosevelt sensed that a coming attack was imminent. Still, they felt it would be in the South Pacific. This assumption meant that there was no need to elevate the defense of their fleets' home base in Pearl Harbor, and unfortunately, for them, this decision would be a fatal error.

It was a beautiful and bright Sunday morning in December, and several blips appeared on the radar at the Opana Radar Site. The two operators, unsure of what they were seeing, contacted their commander and frantically explained that a large group of aircraft had appeared, and they were flying north toward the harbor. The commander informed them that those blips were just the B-17s that were flying in from the States, and there was no need to worry or sound an alarm.

This stroke of luck allowed the attack on Pearl Harbor to remain a surprise. As the clouds parted and the first dive bomber appeared, it was too late. Within minutes, the attack had begun.

The Japanese had planned their attacks in waves, and the first thing they had to do was ensure that none of the American planes would get in the air. The first wave began savagely strafing the airfields. Within half an hour, a handful of aircraft was left to fend off the attack—only six had made it in the air.

The other part of the plan was being executed at the harbor. The ships not fully manned, as many of the sailors were off base attending church, struggled to form some sort of defense against the barrage of bombs and bullets raining down from the sky.

This attack would be devastating in less than 30 minutes. Several of the battleships, including the USS Arizona,

Oklahoma, and California, among others, suffered severe damage or had been sunk.

A little before nine in the morning, the second wave of Japanese fighters was set to begin their attack. This attack was less impactful as the sailors braced for it, but even still, the attack managed to deliver significant damage on top of what had been accomplished in the first wave.

By the time both attacks were done, the U.S. fleet had suffered 3,400 casualties and the loss of many ships and planes. The Japanese had taken significantly less damage. They had lost less than 100 men, a couple of midget submarines, and approximately three dozen aircraft.

The attack, by all accounts, was a stunning victory for the Japanese. Though there was a silver lining for the U.S.: several of their aircraft carriers were not present, and these ships would play a vital role in a later battle for dominance in the Pacific, the Battle of Midway.

Until this attack, American citizens felt that the war was a European problem, and unfortunately for the Japanese, this attack changed that sentiment and allowed the U.S. Government to declare that they were now entering the war.

Hitler's Forces Go to Leningrad

With Operation Barbarossa underway, the Germans knew they had to strike at the heart of the industrial machine of Russia. This factor meant taking Leningrad—now St. Petersburg. Leningrad was the second-largest city in Russia and the industrial heart. Teaming up with the Finnish, the Germans would lay siege to Leningrad for 872 days. Though this siege would last years, the initial few months may well have been the most brutal. By the time the siege ended, the Russian people and military had lost approximately one million lives.

The summer had given the Germans a good bit of success in their campaign, and in September of 1941, they reached one of their prime objectives, Leningrad. This city held more than half of the industrial plants in Russia, and the Germans knew that by seizing it, they would be able to take Russia and end their war with them in no time.

As the German forces pushed west, it was evident to the Russian troops where they were headed, and to save some of their people, a vast majority were evacuated. Even with this evacuation, millions of citizens were left in the city, along with people who had fled the previous attacks from

Germany. Knowing that this was what the Reich intended to target, the Russian leadership co-opted every able-bodied person to help build antitank walls surrounding the city.

In the cold hours of September 8th, the German forces began their siege of Leningrad, and with no access to railways, the city was left unable to replenish their food or supplies. The Germans marched toward the fortifications. Unable to break through, they were stopped by the barricades and soldiers stationed within Leningrad.

The German leadership quickly course-corrected, and on September 9th, began air raids. The targets were strategic military positions as well as the warehouse where the army had stored the food supply for the city. As the planes continued their bombardment, they hit the warehouse, and within minutes, the food storage was consumed in flames.

Now that they had been able to take out those targets, the Germans moved to isolate the city even further. In October, they finished cutting the town off from any means of evacuation or reinforcements. While the Germans did that, their new allies, the Finnish—still desiring revenge after the Russo-Finnish war of a few years earlier—marched from the north down the Karelian Isthmus and lay siege from the north of Leningrad. Once it was surrounded, the Russians in Leningrad only had one path for supplies and escape, and that was across Lake Ladoga.

The siege was locked in place, and all the Germans would have to do is keep the pressure on the Russian forces. German aerial bombardment occurred multiple times daily, not allowing residents and soldiers any time to recoup from previous attacks.

Within Leningrad, things began to take terrible turns. The rations for civilians were cut to one slice of bread a day, and with winter setting in, December would see some of the worst atrocities. The chill blew in, and as winter progressed, the temperatures would drop to below 40. Even in these harsh conditions and with no food, the people were instructed to continue work in the armament factories, some without a roof. To stay warm, books were burnt, and to survive, animals and pets were eaten. Eventually, with no food in sight, people resorted to cannibalism—the Leningrad police even formed a cannibalism division to try to keep order.

Once the lake was frozen, Leningrad could get supplies, but it wasn't enough, and the inhabitants of the city would have to endure this for another two years before the siege would finally end in January of 1944.

Chapter Four
1942: The Tide Turns

The pendulum began to swing in 1942 toward the side of the Allied forces. The inclusion of the U.S. in the war would be a significant part of this. The first troops finding their way into Britain in the early days of 1942 would be a herald for a lot of changes.

Though the European theater would remain firmly in the hands of Germany in the satellite combat zones of North Africa and the pacific, the turn would definitely be in favor of the Allies.

With battles like the Battle of Midway and the Doolittle Raid in the Pacific and the Battle of El Alamein and the beginning of Operation Torch by the Allies in North Africa, it would be a year of bloody conflicts.

On the political front, this year would see the finalization of the "Final Solution" for the Reich at the Wannsee Conference. Elsewhere in the world, other atrocities would be signed into law with the enemy alien program in the U.S. Over the next couple of years, thousands of German, Italian, and Japanese Americans would be sent to internment camps. The fear continued to grow across the globe, and the war itself began to take its toll on both sides.

Wannsee Conference

There had been some movement in what the Reich called the "Jewish Question," but there had not been any finalization, and this troubled Hitler. In July of 1941, Goring had taken the initiative to instruct the leader of the Gestapo and SS, Reinhard Heydrich, to prepare a plan for the "Final Solution."

In January of 1942, near Lake Wannsee, the leaders of the Nazi Party met to hear what Heidrich had concocted. Along with 15 other Nazi leaders—including Adolf Eichmann, the head of Jewish affairs—the plan was laid out in all its horrific detail, and the Wannsee Conference became the final vicious nail in the German persecution and genocidal plan for the Jewish population of Europe.

The list was sent out of the people that Heydrich felt should attend. Along with that summons, Heydrich also sent word to Adolf Eichmann that he needed to produce numbers for the population of Jews in each European country. With all the players in place and the information pulled together, the Wannsee Conference was held on January 20th.

With the crisp January air, the Nazi leadership exited their cars and entered the mansion at 56–58 Am Großen Wannsee. The estate had recently been acquired from Ernst Marlier and was the perfect setting for a day of debate and brainstorming.

Once everyone had arrived, Heydrich began by discussing how the Reich had handled the Jewish community since it had taken over. With the numbers and tactics laid out, he moved on, edging his way to what he felt would be the "Final Solution"—the evacuation of the Jews to the east. As the parties began to talk among themselves, it was clear they understood that it was just a politically correct way to say that the intention of Heydrich was the extermination of the Jewish people.

After an hour of discussing the solution in further detail, Heydrich opened the floor for questions and concerns. Within just an hour and a half, the atrocities that would come to be known as the Holocaust were presented in clear, precise words. The Jewish populations of Europe were to be rounded up and sent east to the labor camps. Those that could work would do so until they could not work any longer, and then they would be sent to the extermination camp where they would be executed by firing squad or gassed. For those deemed unable to work, they would find their way straight to the gas chamber of extermination camps like Chełmno and Auschwitz.

This job and its subsequent renovation of the already existing labor camps were left in the hands of Heinrich Himmler.

By the end of the war, this conference and its "Final Solution" had cost over ten million Jewish lives and left the world scarred forever.

Pacific Theater

After the bombing of Pearl Harbor, the war spread to a new front—the Pacific. The Pacific Theater would be the most significant combat zone in the war as it stretched from the South Pacific into the Indian Ocean and down to Oceania.

This part of WWII was a direct response to Japan's expansionist ideals. To stop the Japanese pushing any further into Asia and taking any more of the islands in the area, the Allied forces had to stop them. With several decisive battles, like the Battle of Midway, in 1942, the Pacific Theater began to take a turn in favor of the Allied forces.

In December of 1941, not only did the Japanese hit the U.S. hard, but also the Allied forces realized that they were intent on taking over the islands and most of southeast Asia. In response to this, the Dutch-exiled government declared war on Japan. The vicious, constant invasions and attacks unnerved the Allies.

In January of 1942, the American, British, Dutch, and Australians got together and helped stave off the attacks. Under the command of General Archibald Wavell, the organization would begin evacuating Dutch citizens and leadership from the shores of the Dutch East Indies to Australia.

In January and February, the Japanese continued their drive, and by the end of February, they had taken control of

Borneo and Sumatra. They would also gain control of the last British foothold in Southeast Asia, Singapore.

One of the most significant conflicts in 1942 was the Battle of Midway, but that wouldn't have even been a battle had it not been for one event—the Doolittle Raid. On April 18th, over half a dozen B-25 bombers filled the skies over the island nation. The president, in response to the attacking of Pearl Harbor, wanted to strike the Japanese hard, but the planes the U.S. had were not long-range and needed to be launched from reasonably close.

With this in mind, the U.S., in conjunction with China, came up with a plan. One of the mighty U.S. aircraft carriers would maneuver themselves to a position roughly 650 miles off mainland Japan—though the initial plan had the ship being anchored 400 miles from the mainland.

The squadron would then launch and drop their bombs. Once the bombs had been dropped, the U.S. pilots would fly over Chinese air space and land. The 16 bombers took off laden with fuel and bombs, and in the bright light of the day, they charted a course for Kobe, Yokosuka, and Osaka. After the bombs were dropped, the pilots turned to continue their flight to the safety of China. However, the extra mileage caused a new problem—none of them would have enough fuel to make it. They still pushed on as far as they could and then did the only thing that they thought they could do: crash their plane or eject. Half of the pilots landed safely but were captured and held captive.

The Japanese knew that the U.S. fleet was using Midway Island as a jumping-off point for their excursions into the South Pacific, and knew by demolishing it, they would be able to take complete control of the waters.

Unfortunately for the Japanese, the U.S. had broken their codes and knew there was a significant attack being planned. Though the U.S. leadership was not sure that the attack would be on Midway, they still began relaying false information over their communications. These communications were a trick because, as the U.S. intelligence continued listening, they heard the communication come over the radio that "AF"—what the Japanese called their target—was short of water.

Now that the U.S. commander, Admiral Chester W. Nimitz, was sure of the target, he and his team could begin planning a counterattack.

Just west of Alaska lay the Aleutian Islands, and as a precursor to the Battle of Midway and potentially a diversionary tactic, the Japanese landed and took these islands. This tactic was meant to draw some of the fleets away from their base at Midway Island. The diversion would hopefully make it easier for the Japanese to gain a victory.

However, the U.S. Navy's ability to decrypt Japanese communications allowed Nimitz the knowledge that the battle had been planned for June 4th or 5th. He did not react the way that the Japanese had expected. Instead, he kept most of the fleet and their planes readily available to make strikes at the incoming Japanese fleet.

The Japanese fleet had been spread out and was approaching from two different points. Having spotted one mass, Nimitz sent a group of B-17 bombers to intercept. Several miles off of Midway, the Japanese Admiral Nobutake Kondō led his ships toward their target, unaware that their location had been compromised. Suddenly, the engines of the Americans B-17s could be heard, and bullets began to strafe the decks of Kondo's ships.

Unfortunately, the Japanese reacted quickly, and very little damage was done to what Nimitz had assumed was the whole of the Japanese fleet. The sun rose over the water, and as it did, another squadron of B-17s took flight from Midway. The objective was once again to stop the advancement of the ships in Kondo's fleet. Once again, this mission came up short.

While the U.S. was busy focusing all their attention on Kondo's ships, Admiral Chūichi Nagumo launched Japan's first wave. From the decks of his four massive aircraft carriers, he sent 108 Japanese planes to attack the base. They buzzed down through the air, dropping bombs and shooting bullets. Within just a few hours, the Japanese had caused massive damage to the base itself.

But they were not successful in crippling the anti-aircraft defenses nor the airfields. As the pilots turned and set their sights to return their aircraft carrier, Nagumo was informed that there would have to be another raid if the Japanese hoped to annihilate the U.S. Naval Base. But the U.S. would not give them any time to make that happen.

Squadrons of aircraft launched from Midway and attempted to strike at the Japanese planes to little avail. The Japanese pilots began to rearm and refuel their planes in preparation for a possible second raid. Then word came back to the Japanese admiral that the U.S. fleet had been spotted approaching Midway from the east. The admiral reacted in haste, knowing that if the fleet made it to Midway, they would never be able to take the base. He changed the plan, and once the pilots had returned from Midway, he planned to lay waste to the approaching fleet.

As the Japanese began to prepare for their assault, they were attacked from out of nowhere by torpedo bombers that had launched from the USS Hornet and Enterprise. Even with the element of surprise, the U.S. could not do much damage.

In fact, the Zero fighters were able to get into the air and take out almost all of the bomber squadrons. Once again, the Japanese returned to their carriers and began to rearm and fuel up, and as they did, another wave of U.S. planes attacked. This time the raid was successful. As the U.S. pilots dove down and dropped their bombs, they successfully managed to hit three of the four Japanese carriers. The fuel and armaments were soon ignited, and the ships were ablaze.

The remaining Japanese carrier, the Hiryū, trying to fend off this attack off, sent two waves of fighter pilots to take out the Yorktown. Though the ship was not damaged beyond repair, the crew of the Yorktown still had to abandon it after the raid by the Japanese planes. But the battle continued as the three other U.S. carriers launched more planes and concentrated on the remaining Japanese ship. As they dive-bombed the ship unleashing their rain of ammunition, the last remaining Japanese carrier decks began to catch fire. The U.S. had succeeded in putting all four carriers out of commission.

Just two days after the Battle of Midway had begun, Admiral Yamamoto, the head of the Japanese fleet, ordered his ships to retreat. This defeat put a kibosh on the Japanese Navy's conquest into the Pacific. Instead, they opted to defend the territory they had already gained.

The Pacific Theater would still have some bloody and devastating battles to come, like the Battle of Guadalcanal. Still, the beginning of the theater clearly started at the Battle of Midway.

North Africa Theater

The Pacific Theater wasn't the only expansion of the conflict. For years, the Germans and Italians had been pushing into North Africa. After all, if they could seize control of the Suez Canal from the British, they would cut off any route of assistance for the Russians and hold control of the waterways to the gulf—a significant transportation route.

They would garner control over raw materials like oil. This campaign was meant to cut off the head of the mighty British Empire. By keeping them from being able to connect with their colonial hubs in the Middle East as well as in Asia, the Axis would gain further control.

In 1942, Erwin Rommel, the German leader of the North African campaign, would start a second push deeper into North Africa. During the first part of the year, the gains would be significant for the Axis powers, eventually though, the Allied forces would launch Operation Torch and begin to turn the tides.

In 1941, the German General Erwin Rommel had landed in Tripoli, Libya, with his newly-formed military unit known as the Afrika Corps. Hitler had answered the call of help from his friend from the south, Mussolini, and had created this unit specifically to help the Italian dictator gain more ground in North Africa.

In the end, Rommel would end up the head of the entire North African campaign. The British had been occupying Libya, and for months, the two forces had fought back and forth, trying to establish dominance and remove the other from the territory.

The key was Tobruk! This port city had been under British control for almost two years, and Rommel knew that capturing it would give the Axis the upper hand. After months of back and forth, Rommel decided to turn his attention to the port and, in late June of 1942, used his Panzer Divisions to execute a raid and devastating attacks on the battlements surrounding the British 8th Army's stronghold.

With swift and ferocious attacks, Rommel succeeded in pushing this division back, not Egypt. Then all that was left was to take out the 11th Indian Brigade housed inside the walls of Tobruk. Rommel knew it would take more than just his panzers. With the aid of dive bombers from the Luftwaffe and massive artillery barrages, Rommel devastated the Allied forces.

After hours of constant attack, Genera Henrik Klopper was forced to order his troops to stand down and surrender. Rommel had taken the port along with prisoners and supplies, and for this, Hitler honored him with one of the highest rewards, the field marshal baton. Rommel, unsatisfied with this victory, pushed on further into North Africa on his mission to take the Suez Canal.

For several days, Rommel would push his way into Egypt, but this would prove challenging. On June 30th, Rommel reached the British defensive line at El Alamein. The only way to reach his goal was to break this defensive line, and feeling emboldened by his recent victory, Rommel attacked the line but found it nearly impenetrable. Having failed at the first attack, Rommel pulled back and began to rethink his strategy.

Meanwhile, the British 8th, led by General Claude Auchinleck, fired back with a strike of their own. Having gained nothing, the two forces soon found themselves in a battle of attrition. The British troops had stopped Rommel dead in his tracks, and for the next two weeks, the first battle of Amiens continued with little to no gain but plenty of losses.

Though Auchinleck had succeeded in holding the line, he had failed to defeat the Germans, and the British command made the bold move to remove him from power. His replacement, though, would end up dead, and this would leave control over the British forces at El Alamein in the hands of Field Marshal Bernard Montgomery.

With the fighting reaching a stalemate, the newly-appointed Montgomery took the time to build up the size of his army, knowing that Rommel wouldn't back down easily. The field marshal would use the defensive line already built up to prevent the German forces from being able to use their most valuable piece of equipment—the Panzer tank.

The El Alamein defensive line had been designed using the Qattara depression as its southern border so that mobilization of mechanized troops wasn't possible. This strategic design gave the British the advantage as their strengths lay in their artillery and infantry.

For two months, Montgomery built up his forces, and by mid-October, had forces double that of Rommel in both men and tanks, not to mention the air. Rommel knew that Montgomery was up to something, and seeing the equipment and troops amass, built up his defenses as well.

This defensive build-up was done by the dispersal and placement of over a thousand different antitank and antipersonnel mines. Rommel expected this to slow the

British 8th Army down enough to allow him and his troops to get the upper hand.

With all the plans made and the troops set, Montgomery was ready to execute his strategy. Under the light of a nearly full moon, 800 guns began firing on the German camp. Under cover of fire from their side, the British sappers—also known as Royal Engineers—moved into the field between the two armies and began to remove the mines carefully laid by Rommel's men.

With some of the area cleared, the British infantry and tanks moved into position and advanced on the Germans. The Germans, surprised by the sudden attack, sprang into action. Though the British were lying in wait left and right, the battle seemed to drag on for hours. The speed of the oncoming British forces was slowed as they had to wait for their sappers to clear the fields as they went, and this allowed Rommel to mount several counterattacks.

The German mines that were partially taken care of still managed to do their job and knock out several of the British tanks. That, coupled with the highly accurate aim of the German troops when it came to anti-tank weapons, allowed the Germans and Italians to make some effective counterattacks.

Even still, the infantry comprised of British as well as Australian and New Zealand units were able to make their way through and open up paths that the British capitalized on successfully. For ten days, this battle waged on, and by November 2nd, Rommel sent word that the battle was lost.

Hitler refused to admit defeat and ordered Rommel to stand his ground, but Rommel, unwilling to sacrifice his troops, began to withdraw, leaving the Italian units there to fight the British alone.

The second battle of El Alamein was the shot across the bow from the Allied forces. Just six days later, Operation Torch would be launched. With the landings in Algeria and Morocco, the Axis powers in Northern Africa were caught between a rock and a hard place.

With the two allied fronts in both the east and the west pushing toward each other, eventually, by the end of 1943, North Africa would be reclaimed, and the German and Italian forces were driven back to mainland Europe or captured. This victory would allow the Allied forces to concentrate on landings in Western Europe like the one that would spell the beginning of the end for the Nazi rule—the Battle of Normandy.

Russia Under Attack!

The German conquest of Russian territories continued into 1942. This year ended with one of the bloodiest battles of the entire campaign—the Battle of Stalingrad. With most of the Ukraine and Belarus in their control, Germany turned to the south and marched on to Stalingrad.

The Germans had failed to capture Moscow and still lay siege to Leningrad but wanted to capture another of the Red Amy's industrial hubs. By marching and conquering Stalingrad, they would deal a blow to Stalin tactically as well as strategically as they would be able to block any transportation up the Volga. Plus, Hitler felt that capturing the city named after the Russian leader would be considered a boon, propaganda-wise.

To begin the assault psychologically before a German soldier set foot on that land, Hitler made it known that when the Germans took the city, all men would be killed, and the women were taken to one of the labor camps in the west. This declaration riled Stalin up, and he decreed that every male citizen that could hold a gun would, and they would defend the city until they could no longer.

After a long march, the German 6th Army found their way to the outskirts of Stalingrad, and on August 23rd, the battle began. The Russian leadership, having experienced the German strategic plans in Leningrad, knew that the first target would be the food stores and livestock. As the German forces were slowed down by several attacks on the way to the city, the Russian troops had been moved from Stalingrad.

The Russians, however, did not evacuate their people. This maneuver was a tactical ploy hoping that the presence of civilians would push their troops to defend the city with greater vigor. But the Russian forces protecting the city would need more than inspiration to survive the onslaught that the Germans brought with them.

Starting with artillery barrages and air raids by the Luftwaffe, the Germans quickly gained the upper hand. After the first few days had passed, the Volga was rendered useless. Its water became cluttered with the remains of many commercial boats. The air raid would continue for the duration of the battle, and by the end of August, the city was in a desperate situation.

As fall continued and the air became crisper, the Luftwaffe would not let up, and the Russian people and soldiers of Stalingrad had to think outside the box. The civilians soon became part of the war effort. Anyone not working on necessary war-related items was drafted to fight the battle with their own guns, and the women even used to dig trenches.

The Russians would see the most substantial losses, and yet they fought on for the love of their country and fear of the repercussions of surrender. Finally, as the resources dwindled, the Russian leadership began to send reinforcements. Snipers began to set up on building tops, and both sides would pick each other off.

In the mountains surrounding the city, two forces set up camp and began launching countermeasures. As winter began to move closer, the Russian troops gradually moved into place, forming a circle around the German armies in effect, creating a blockade. Once the blockade was in place and winter set in, the Germans all but lost the battle. Without access to supplies and reinforcements, the German soldiers were left to their own devices, and many would starve before the battle was over.

The Battle of Stalingrad would continue through the end of 1942, and not come to an end until February of 1943.

The cost to both sides was immense, and the Russian victory here was a significant turn on the Eastern front of the war.

Chapter Five
1943: Alliances & Defeats

In 1943, the cracks in the Reich's armor began to widen as they suffered many defeats. On all fronts, the Axis powers began to lose ground from the North Africa territory, where the forces surrendered in Tunisia to tides turning in the Battle of the Atlantic.

Black May would see Admiral Donitz having to recall many of his Seawolf brigades from the open waters, thanks to the Bletchley code breakers. Italy would fall, and the Pacific Theater would see victories for the Allies at Guadalcanal.

On the Russian front, the Battle of Kursk would seal the Germans' fate in their Eastern campaign. This, combined with the surrender of the Germans at Stalingrad and the Warsaw Ghetto uprising, showed that the German war machine was finally starting to stutter.

All of the victories and successful defenses would lead to the leaders of the three main powers—U.S., Britain, and Russia—meeting at Tehran to discuss the Allied invasion of France.

Casablanca & Tehran Conference

There would be a more intensified unification of the strategies and tactics of the Allied forces in 1943. This unification would be done by two major conferences that bookended the year. These conferences would give way to the military movement and strategies that would bring the Reich to their knees and put the final nail in their coffin.

In January, the Casablanca Conference would lay out plans for the final push into North Africa, cement the need for Britain and the U.S. to help the Russians, put bombers over the cities of Germany, and define a way to win the war in the Atlantic. The Tehran Conference would also set out plans of attack—including the Allied invasion of France—for the coming year—1944—as well as discuss the political and geographical terms of what post-war Europe may look like after an Allied win.

With the conflict well underway in the North African Theater, Churchill and Roosevelt began to correspond and discuss the course the war would take in the coming months. The two nations' leaders were at odds about how to continue, and it was decided that they should meet to hammer out the details. But first, the location and security had to be addressed along with the inclusion of the other significant power—Russia.

A message was sent to Stalin, inviting him to the conference. Stalin declined though, as he was needed to deal with both Leningrad as well as Stalingrad. The parties all lined up, the security became the focus, and this fell on the shoulders of George S. Patton. Patton knew that the location needed to be easily monitored, and he chose the Anfa Hotel.

This meeting would be the first time that Roosevelt had left the U.S. during the war, and it was to be a long and arduous journey. It would take him several days to arrive in Morocco.

Churchill, on the other hand, arrived there rather quickly, and as soon as both touched ground, they were hurried to the hotel. Around the hotel, Patton had established a one-mile squared compound. Once everyone was settled, the conference could begin.

On January 14th, the two leaders sat down for the first time at the conference and started the debate on what was to be done. As the two leaders bantered back and forth, the first topic was the need to help the Soviet Union. The two quickly came to the agreement that they both needed to send equipment and supplies to ensure the Russians kept the pressure on in the east. They also promptly decided on the bombing of key strategic points within the borders of Germany as well as how they would proceed to guarantee a win in the Atlantic.

As the conference continued, the subject of how to allocate forces in Europe and the Pacific became very time-consuming. Churchill and his military command felt that the focus should be on Germany. However, the U.S. leadership was afraid that if the Allies reallocated resources from the Pacific that the Japanese would continue their expansion and consolidate their forces into a streamlined fighting force that could end up being unstoppable.

What would happen after the vestry in North Africa was also a note of contention? The U.S. generals and the president agreed that the forces should move north into Sicily but did not want to do so until there was a definitive plan to strike the killing blow to Hitler and his Nazi regime.

Churchill had a plan already in mind. In his passionate tone, he detailed how the Allied forces would strike at the soft underbelly of the German Reich by pushing into southern Europe, starting with Italy. By taking out Mussolini and liberating Italy, the Germans would have no other choice but to move their troops to the south to protect their borders. These troops would inevitably have to come from France and the Eastern front.

This reallocation of forces would weaken the line and allow for an invasion to go via the English Channel. After ten days of debating and negotiating, the two nations came to a decision, and on January 24th, reporters were summoned to the Anfa Hotel. The press corps was shocked as the top brass of both the British and the Americans filed out on to the stage and then gasped as Roosevelt and Churchill entered the room. Patton had done an excellent job, and no one had known that the conference was even going on.

Once everyone was in the room, Roosevelt stepped forward and began to address the press. The words echoed through the room as Roosevelt described the intention of the conference and some key points that were discussed. Then in a bold and confident voice, he talked of peace and how the world would only find it with the total elimination of the German and Japanese powers.

Roosevelt went on to elaborate that this meant the unconditional surrender of the leadership of Germany, Italy, and Japan. He did not seek the destruction of the population; instead, the destruction of the ideologies that had driven the people to commit the horrific offenses. The conference had defined the movements for the next year and moved the focus to Europe and the Mediterranean while still giving the U.S. enough to focus on the Pacific Theater as well.

Eleven months after the Casablanca Conference, another vital meeting would occur, this time in Tehran. On November 28th, Stalin, Churchill, and Roosevelt would come together to discuss the second front. The British and the Americans would launch an invasion of France, opening up the Western front, and Stalin would continue to deliver devastating defeats on the Eastern front. Stalin, in fact, would be the biggest proponent of the two other Allied forces beginning their preparations for the invasion of France.

For four days, the three leaders and their command would discuss the preparations as well as many other political problems. Stalin was firm in his belief that the German-Soviet Non-aggression Pact, as well as the Russo-Finnish Treaty, should be upheld and that the lands gained by the Soviet Union during it should remain in Russian hands. He also pushed his plan to retain the Baltic Coast that came with the East Prussian state.

For the most part, these topics were answered, and all parties involved seemed uncertain of what was the right course of action. However, Roosevelt had an area that he fervently disagreed with Stalin—Poland. Roosevelt wanted to give the country back and allow the exiled government to return to their duties. Stalin, on the other hand, distrusted and despised the Polish leaders. However, when all was said and done, they had a concrete answer: Iran. It would have its own will and determine its economic future once the war was over.

On December 1st, the three leaders appeared in front of the press and declared their intentions. Peace would rest on their shoulders and that of the United Nations of the world. That together, the terror of war would come to an end.

Once the conference was over, Stalin returned to Russia to begin his preparations for a new push further into German-occupied areas. Churchill and Roosevelt moved their meeting to Cairo and began discussing the leadership and needs of Operation Overlord.

In the end, Dwight D. Eisenhower—a future U.S. president—was chosen as the general to lead the operation, and the stage was set for a bloody and long 1944.

Russia & Germany

Stalingrad—see Russia Under Attack (p. 81)—had waged on for months when the new year rolled around. By late January, the harsh Russian winter and the counteroffensive launched by General Zhukov had the German forces reeling.

The Italians and Romanians that were fighting alongside the Germans had already given up, and General von Paulus of the German 6th Army held on. With limited access to new supplies and reinforcements, Hitler knew that the general struggled with the orders to hold the line. To give him a little inspiration, Hitler promoted him to field marshal, and in a robust communication, reminded him that no German field marshal had ever surrendered.

This promotion kept Paulus motivated, and he pushed his men on through winter. Loss of life that winter was immense. Soldiers were dying from the harsh weather, from starvation, and from the continuous and vicious attacks of the Russians defending their city.

January would bring some of the most devastating defeats for the German forces. Of these, the loss of the last airport under German control was the most significant. This loss would mean that no more supplies were coming, and the German soldiers would have to use what they had, which wasn't much. Unable to keep the fight going, the German troops in the southern sector of Stalingrad surrendered to the Russian forces on January 31st.

It would take two more days for the rest of the forces to realize the fight was over and surrender to the Russians. The captives of Stalingrad, which was about 90,000 men, were all sent to Soviet POW camps and would spend the rest of the war there. This battle turned the tide and set the Germans up for defeat after defeat—including the one at the Battle of

Kursk—as the Russians pushed them back further and further.

The Kursk salient was one of the most crucial strategic holding points of the Eastern front of WWII, and Hitler understood this—so did his generals. In the early part of March, Field Marshal Erich von Manstein wanted to continue his momentum and take Kursk. He had demolished the resistance both in Belgorod and Kharkiv and was close enough to the bulge that he felt his men could comfortably ride the wave and conquer the vital city of Kursk easily. But the remainder of the Wehrmacht leadership wanted to delay that course of action so they could prepare adequately. He was outvoted, and the German forces began their preparations.

Within a few months, they would stockpile equipment, munitions, as well as amass over half a million men near the Kursk. This sudden lack of movement and the amassment of troops and equipment tipped the Germans' hat, and the Soviets began rapidly producing artillery, tanks, and planes. At the same time that it took the Germans to ready themselves, the Russians were able to do the same, which set the stage for an epic, bloody battle.

The delay in execution of the attack on the Kursk Bulge was enough to have some of the Wehrmacht's generals to become gun shy when it came to the implementation of Operation Citadel. Worried that they had given the Russians enough time to plan for counterattacks, there were several of the German military leadership that pleaded with Hitler to forget the idea. But Hitler would hear nothing of it and planned to move on Kursk. The operation was set to be executed on May 3rd, but Hitler felt that that was still too soon and wanted to postpone the action just a bit.

The German leader wanted to ensure better weather and that his new and improved Panther and Tiger tanks could be delivered to the front line. This delay allowed the Russians even more time to fortify their lines of defense. The defensive fortifications included laying mines, building tank traps, and digging over 2,500 miles of trenches. The German WWII battle strategy was that of Blitzkrieg, and without surprise, this tactic was all but useless.

Finally, after months of preparations and waiting, in the early morning of July 5th, the operation was launched. Lying in wait among the wheat fields of the area around Kursk, both the Soviet Army and the Germans began to push forward. However, before the Germans could get their initial salvo off, the Soviets sent a blast of artillery fire their way. There were panic and shock!

The Russian attack halted the Germans' advance. However, the Germans were able to quickly regain focus and begin their assault. The battle started with artillery fire focused on the north and south points of the bulge. Once significant damage was done, the infantry began to move in, aided by the Luftwaffe. The Russian Air Force (the VVS) tried to mount an opposition but were not as skilled as the Luftwaffe, and this maneuver was unsuccessful.

Where the Soviets had the upper hand was their defensive line. The preparation over the past few months had allowed them to set up many traps that all but neutralized the German tanks from moving into the bulge. In fact, just five days after the initiation of Operation Citadel, the Russians had stopped the German 9th Army's advance.

On July 10th, Hitler and his leadership would receive news of Allied troops landing in Sicily. With the stalemate in Kursk, Hitler decided that it was much more important to protect his southern borders from Allied forces making their way to it and reallocated many of his Panzer Division to Italy. This news all but spelled the end of Operation Citadel.

The German forces tried to execute several small attacks against Russian soldiers in the south. Still, with so little numbers, the Russians were able to defend themselves and come out victorious. For the remainder of July, the Russians executed several counteroffensives, and by July 24th, they had broken through the German lines and had the Germans on the run.

Allies Invade Italy

Mussolini had built his fascist dictatorship but never achieved the glory of the Roman Empire like he had set out to do. By 1943, several groups were opposing his tyranny and wanted peace with the Allies. On July 10th, the Allied forces landed in Sicily and were able to take a foothold on the small island.

Led by Patton, the Allied forces soon worked their way to mainland Italy. In just under a month, Patton and his Allied troops had made it all the way to Messina. It wasn't long before word of the occupation found its way to Rome, and Mussolini's government buckled.

On July 25th, Mussolini resigned and found himself arrested the next day. That same day, Marshal Petro Badoglio took control of the government, and out of the prying eyes of the public, began peace negotiations with the allied forces.

On September 3rd, the rest of the Allied troops landed, and the Italian Government soon issued a public surrender.

On September 8th, the Italian Government officially declared its surrender.

In terms of the peace agreement, the Italian Government agreed to help the Allies expel the German presence in return for leniency. However, they did not expel the German forces soon enough. A month after imprisoning Mussolini, German commandos extracted him from prison, and he was immediately put in place as the head of the Northern Italian state, which in essence, was just a Nazi-run Italian city-state.

It would not be until spring of the following year that Mussolini would meet his end at the hands of his opposition.

Black May – Tide Turns in The Battle of The Atlantic

The Casablanca Conference covered a lot of ground, but one of the most important topics was the Battle of the Atlantic. For the last few years, German U-boats had been reigning terror on the Allied fleets, and there had to be something done about it.

Both Roosevelt and Churchill, along with their top military leaders, agreed that something had to be done and decided that a significant naval presence accompanied by the aid of the air force would be the only way to move forward. In April, the new tactics were put to use, and along with excellent weather and improved radar equipment, the Allied forces were able to build a presence and deliver a crushing blow to the German Naval Forces.

The new initiative would be executed by the new Western Approaches Commander, Admiral Max Horton. The campaign would be performed by hunter-killer groups comprised of aircraft escort carriers and fast escorts. These troupes would operate in tandem, and instead of suppressing the U-boats, they would go on the attack. Between April and May, over 50 U-boats had been damaged or destroyed.

The month of May would be the most significant loss for the German Navy, and Admiral Donitz knew that he had to make a decision. Would he press on with the tonnage war they had been fighting, or pull his resources back to restructure their tactics and continue with the U-boat campaign?

This decision was not an easy one, as Donitz knew that continuing the U-boat campaign would lead to losses beyond what they had previously experienced. In essence, every U-boat that left the port would be sent out on a suicide mission. He needed the opinion of his fellow sailors and met with several of them. After the meeting, Donitz knew what he had to do. Despite the loss of life and vessels, the U-boat campaign had to continue. This decision would appease the Fuhrer and keep the submarine service moving forward. It would also keep the Allies busy patrolling several thousand miles of water and keep tons of resources busy.

Donitz also felt that maintaining a U-boat campaign would allow the submariners to understand the Allies' new tactics. By gaining a grasp of these tactics, the German U-boats would be able to develop countermeasures to address them. This decision, however, did not sit well with the men stationed on the U-boats, and many began to distrust Donitz's decision, feeling he had finally fallen into the arms of the Fuhrer's madness.

Chapter Six

1944: Beginnings of Liberation

The plan that was set forth at the Tehran Conference came to fruition in 1944. From the invasion of France on D-Day to the liberation of Italy, the Allies on the Western front saw quite a bit of success.

On the Eastern front, the Russians pushed into Poland and Belarus. The Pacific Theater would see the only positive gain by the Axis powers as Japan moved further into China. However, the Japanese would begin to lose ground in the islands, losing Saipan and struggling to maintain the Philippines.

This year would be the year of the Allies beginning to liberate cities and countries that had been subjected to

German rule for the past several years. The beaches of Normandy would be stormed, and the greatest and bloodiest battle of the war—the Battle of the Bulge—would begin.

Assassination Attempt

Hitler had risen to power through diplomatic means. Still, after seizing power, he turned the democratic government of Germany into a dictatorship, and that didn't sit well with some of the elite within the leadership. Many of the German military and political leaders had no problem with his ideological war but tactically felt that he was leading Germany into destruction by fighting on two fronts and tarnishing the German people's reputation and pride.

These individuals may have been in the minority—some 200 individuals involved in the plot to assassinate Hitler—but nonetheless, they held their ground and hatched over two dozen plots to eliminate the Fuhrer. One of the last may have been the one that came the closest to achieving their agenda.

Operation Valkyrie was executed on July 20th. The plan was simple: eliminate Hitler by placing a bomb in a meeting and then after his death, arrest and seize power back of Berlin. Things did not go as planned.

Though late to join the resistance, Claus von Stauffenberg was chosen to implement the mission. He had access to the Fuhrer as the chief of the army reserve and would, in the minds of the conspirators, be able to blend in. He was all but willing to take the job on as he had begun to see Hitler as a maniacal madman and knew he needed to be stopped.

The date was set for July 20th, 1944, and the place had been chosen as well. Hitler was gathering his elite together to discuss future military movements at the Berchtesgaden. The Gestapo got wind of a potential attack being planned, and Himmler urged Hitler to move to a more secure location. To ensure the safety of the Fuhrer, Himmler suggested the Wolf's Lair. This bunker in Prussia was virtually unknown to most people, except for the elite trusted military leaders and the inner circle of Hitler.

The new location set the Gestapo at ease, and its leader felt the conspirators would be unable to carry out their plan. Himmler's intel was wrong, and Stauffenberg was able to infiltrate the meeting. As the meeting began, Stauffenberg entered the room casually, holding a briefcase. He slowly, and without being noticed, set the briefcase down and left the room as fast as he had come. The drop had gone unnoticed, and the conference began. Hitler, along with several military leaders, were hunched over a map of the Eastern front, trying to figure out how to preserve their foothold. As they began to move around the map, one of the military leaders, Colonel Heinz Brandt, trying to get a better look at the map, kicked the briefcase and moved it away from the table—saving the Fuhrer's life without knowing it.

A little past 12:30 the afternoon, the bomb exploded. The bunker filled with smoke and debris took a few minutes to clear. When it did, Hitler stood tall, wounded, but alive. The four others that were in the war room with him lay dead among the rubble.

The German leader had burns all over his body, a burst eardrum, and one of his arms was temporarily paralyzed. Once the shock had worn off, he continued with his day. He had important business to attend to, and he would not let a mere assassination attempt keep him from it. (This included a visit from some of his comrades from the south, Benito Mussolini.)

Stauffenberg was on his way back to Berlin when the bomb went off. Operation Valkyrie was a go, and they had to move quickly to ensure they were able to take control of the central government in Berlin. Stauffenberg and his partner in crime, General Friedrich Olbricht, initiated their coup by arresting the reserve army's commander. Once he was in custody, they sent out orders for the military to begin seizing several government buildings. But then Goring issued a statement about the assassination attempt and assured the German people that Hitler was alive and fine.

The commander of the reserves, General Fromm, was released by the conspirators thinking he would join the coup, but that was a deadly miscalculation. Fromm turned on the two military men, and they were arrested and killed that day. The next few weeks would be spent rooting out the conspirators and arresting or executing them. The conspiracy was deep, and by the time the investigation was done, Hitler had not only found the 200 men directly in charge of the plot but also many more, including the highly respected Erwin Rommel.

The Gestapo and Hitler gave the traitors a choice: to be arrested and executed or to end their own life. Rommel opted for suicide. Hitler and his propaganda machine would use this failed attempt as a way to show the German people that fate had left him alive to ensure the dominance and success of the German people. This failed attempt would bolster morale but only very briefly as the Reich was about to take some severe losses and begin to fall apart.

The Liberation of Paris

Paris had been in the hands of the Germans for four years and had seen some severe devastation. With the taking of the beach at Normandy, the Allied forces had a foothold to work from to retake France and the lowland countries. Paris was on tap to be liberated, and by mid-August, the troops had worked their way to the outskirts. With news of the Allied forces approaching, the resistance fighters still within Paris rose and began to attack the German forces.

A little over a week after arriving on the outskirts, Paris was once again in Allied hands. Though things could have been very different had Eisenhower not been convinced to go ahead with the operation, but wait for reinforcements.

Eisenhower, at his command base near Normandy, was being advised to surround the city and simply wait for more troops and equipment to arrive. However, on August 21st, Charles de Gaulle, upon visiting, was informed of this plan and was shocked. Paris was ripe for the taking, and by waiting, they would allow the Germans to craft strategic plans and send word for help, the French general explained.

The discussion continued, and de Gaulle relayed more intelligence to Eisenhower about the strength of the communist party within Paris. If they did not move now, they would fail, but they may also be leaving the future of the French Government in the hands of communists. In the end, the heated conversation ended with de Gaulle kindly informing Eisenhower that even if the Americans and British did not move to liberate Paris, he would instruct the French 2nd Armored Division to enter the city on their own.

Convinced that de Gaulle was right, Eisenhower began the operation the very next day. With Paris surrounded, he ordered an infantry division to move from the south and a tank division to move into the city from the north.

The German forces, led by General Dietrich von Choltitz, were spread too thin to defend against this attack adequately. The German troops were fighting the resistance that had risen once the Allied forces surrounded Paris.

Word came down that it was becoming evident that the Allies would march on to Paris to reinforce the defense and to get ready to raise the city to the ground if the partners looked like they were going to win. With this order, Choltitz sent his troops out to begin planting explosives on all major bridges and around many of the iconic landmarks throughout Paris. He would later defy this order as he wanted to preserve his name and not be known as the monster that destroyed one of Europe's most beloved cities.

The Allied troops of the 2nd Armored Division rolled into the outskirts of Paris and were quickly greeted with heavy artillery fire. Eventually, though, they plowed through the German defenses and made their way across the Seine. Once the armored division made it into the suburbs, the people left their homes and showered them with gifts they had saved from the German oppression and were grateful.

That same day, the French 4th Infantry pushed into Paris as well. By late evening on August 24th, the Allied troops had reached the Hotel de Ville, and the liberation of Paris was all but complete.

Throughout the night, German resistance began to lose steam, and eventually, most of the force surrendered. As the light of morning began to glisten across the city, the Allied forces swept the rest of the city for remaining pockets of German resistance. But the Allies had not yet captured the commander of the German occupation of Paris. That would not come until later in the day when Choltitz was arrested and formally signed a surrender. This document put a provisional government in place led by General Charles de Gaulle.

Significant Battles of The European Theater

Some of the biggest and most memorable battles on the European front would happen in 1944. From the storming of the Beaches in Normandy to the final liberation of Italy, the Western front was led to victory by the British and Americans.

On the Eastern front, major battles at Minsk and the final lift of the siege of Leningrad would leave the Russians even more in charge of the way of the war on the Eastern front.

In June of 1944, the Russians knew it was time to remove the German presence in Belarus. Over the three-year occupation, the Nazis devastated the small Baltic nation. Hundreds of cities and villages were demolished, and millions of the Jewish population had been killed or taken to the concentration camps in Germany and Poland.

To do this, it would take an accelerated and well-timed operation that would take out the strategic operations center in Minsk. Removing this post, the Belarusians and Russians would regain control of the Baltic nation and be one step closer to pushing into Germany to end the reign of the Third Reich. This strategic operation was code-named Operation Bagration and would become known to the Soviets as the Great Patriotic War.

As the moon lifted into the sky that warm June 19th, the Nazis were in for quite the surprise. Unbeknownst to them, several groups of Belarusian resistance fighters had carefully placed explosions at key tactical transportation hubs. One by one, thunderous explosions rocked the countryside, and when the smoke cleared, not only were the German soldiers surprised, but many of the routes they use to get supplies and fuel were now out of commission.

A week later, after the Germans began to feel the weight of no reinforcements or resupplying of their needed goods, two Belarusian units, the 1st and 3rd Divisions, converged on the German troops in Minsk. Both of these units were outfitted with fast-moving Russian T-34 and KV-1 tanks. Germans troops and tank divisions flanked Minsk, and the job of the 2nd Army was to attack the German forces that were retreating into the city limits of Minsk.

Along with these military units, the landscape of Belarus required a new support unit to be created. This unit would be responsible for protecting bridges and river crossings from being destroyed or seized. This tactic would allow for the Belarusian forces to move freely without delay, due to course correction. Over the first few days, the Belarusian authorities would push toward Minsk, liberating cities like Borisov, Polotsk, Minsk, and Slutsk.

By the evening of July 2nd, the Belarusian forces had reached Minsk and began the final leg of Operation Bagration. From all sides, Belarusian and Soviet troops moved into the city. The conflicts were brutal, and the German forces, with very little hope, were finally overcome by midday. The town had been liberated, and word was sent back to the capital, Moscow, where the leadership and people celebrated the freedom of the Belarusian people from the fascist German occupation.

On July 5th, the Marshal of the Soviet Union, Vasilevsky, made his way to Minsk and officially liberated the city. Over the next few days, the remaining Germans continued to fight, but in the end, their commander made his way to the Soviet lines and surrendered.

On the Western front, there were significant victories, but none could meet the devastation and success of the Battle of Normandy. After the U.S. entered the war in 1941, they and their allies, the British, immediately began talking about the idea of mounting a significant attack over the British Channel. The conversation was intense, but the actual strategic planning of the campaign was not started until 1943.

As the news of expanding forces and troop movements found its way to Hitler, he moved the renowned General Erwin Rommel into the command of the Nazi forces of northern France. Hitler and his military leadership had already begun defense preparations on the coast, and Rommel's mission was to complete the 2,400-mile defense system known as the Atlantic Wall.

The Atlantic Wall was a series of bunkers, minefields, and beach and water obstructions. In January of 1944, the operation would receive a new commander, future president and war hero Dwight D. Eisenhower. Eisenhower, along with the British commander, Bernard Montgomery, moved to execute the attack by June 5th.

The six months leading up to the campaign were crucial and required to atone of subterfuge. The whole attack relied on the German military command and troops believing the attack was going to come at one location when, in fact, the Allied forces would hit them from another. The site chosen was an obvious one—the Pas-de-Calais.

This location was the narrowest point of the English Channel, but in order to keep the Nazis guessing, their other potential locations for the landing were leaked as well. On top of the miscommunication over the radio, Eisenhower and Montgomery placed fake equipment in critical positions for the Germans' aerial reconnaissance to see. These tactics, coupled with the "nonexistent army" commanded by Patton, were all relayed through double agents and those fake communications.

With all the pieces in place, the Allied command finalized the day. The attack would come on June 5th. In the early morning hours of June 5th, Eisenhower's meteorologist reported that the weather would clear, and Eisenhower delayed troop movements.

True to the report, later in the day, a break in the storm came, and Operation Overlord was a go. Throughout the rest of the day, supplies and troops moved into place. As the sun began to rise on June 6th, air support had already dropped thousands of soldiers behind enemy lines, and at precisely 6:30 in the morning, the invasion of the beaches began.

With little to no resistance, the British and Canadians took three of the beaches. The Americans took Utah beach but ran into massive resistance. The day came with heavy casualties on both sides, but when the smoke cleared, the beaches of Normandy were almost entirely under allied control. It would take another five days before the allied forces entirely occupied them, and they could begin the push into northern France.

Allies Gain Ground in The Pacific

The Pacific Theater saw plenty of movement as well. The Allied forces would retake Burma and New Guinea and see significant gains in the Mariana Islands.

The year 1944 would also see vital progress in the conflict on Japanese soil. From air raids on Okinawa to the bombing of aircraft factories near Tokyo, the U.S. and Allied fleets began to raise the stakes even higher. Through the winter and spring, they would push deeper into mainland Asia while taking island after island.

The first bombing raid since the failed Doolittle raid would be executed, and two of the battles that could be called a turning point in this part of the war—the Battle of the Philippine Sea and the Battle of Leyte Gulf—would go down in the history books.

Saipan, Tinian, and Guam were important tactical bases for Japan. That made the Mariana Islands a strategic target that the U.S. and their Allied friends in the Philippine Sea could not pass up.

On June 15th, the first shots were fired, making the Allied forces' plans known as marines landed on Saipan and began to fight the Japanese stationed there. The Japanese knew that any further infiltration of U.S. forces on the Mariana Islands could be a crushing blow to their expansionist agenda. Admiral Jisaburō Ozawa was sent to intercept the 5th Fleet that was on its way for support.

Within the range of the fleet led by Admiral Raymond Spruance, Ozawa launched 430 airplanes into the sky with the mission of annihilating the 5th Fleet. However, this would be a suicide mission for most of these pilots. The U.S. fleet had already picked up the Japanese planes on radar and was prepared for the attack.

One by one, the Japanese planes were shot out of the sky. By the time the "battle" was over, 300 Japanese aircraft had been taken out as well as two Japanese aircraft carriers. The Americans had suffered minor losses, and the fleet was still geared up for anything.

This readiness would include the second attack on the Japanese by a second American aircraft carrier commanded by Admiral Mitscher. This was only possible due to the overconfidence of the Japanese leader as Ozawa assumed that all of his planes had made it safely to their destination on Guam. This assuredness would be his downfall as the second aircraft launched their own attack and took out even more planes as well as another aircraft carrier.

After this decisive victory, the Americans were set to take the Mariana Islands and put a damper on Japan's tactical capabilities in the Pacific Theater. This battle would be the gateway to the marines landing and taking Saipan back as well as Gaum and Tinian. The crushing defeats received one after the other would lead Premier Hideki Tojo to abdicate their position.

The battle for the Mariana Islands and the Philippines had begun with the Battle of the Philippine Sea, but it would come to an end with the Battle of Leyte Gulf. The battle for the Philippines would start with the invasion of Leyte island. Once word reached the Japanese command of a U.S. landing on the island, they readied their fleet and deployed them quickly.

Japan sat in a precarious position with the distribution of their forces as well as their fuel resources. The fleets moved from training in the water near Taiwan, leaving them open for attack and easy pickings for the U.S. forces in the area.

As one of the Japanese fleets sailed toward the Philippines, the Japanese military command ordered it to break off and navigate into the Leyte Gulf through the Surigao Strait. Admiral Kurita Takeo followed the orders and captained his fleet straight into a position where their T was crossed and demolished by the U.S. forces lying in wait.

The Japanese cruiser division tried to follow suit but, realizing what had happened, quickly veered away from the gulf. Kurita maneuvered the rest of his fleet to the north and managed to draw the U.S. 3rd Fleet, commanded by Admiral William F. Halsey, away from their position, which left the San Bernardino Strait clear.

The Japanese fleet rushed through the straight but still came under attack from both the air and the U.S. submarines stationed there. Admiral Kurt moved on but came so close to Leyte Gulf that he encountered several attacks and was eventually driven from the water surrounding the Philippines.

Chapter Seven
1945: The Final Conflicts

The final year of the war would bring to light the horrors committed by the Nazis as concentration camps began to be liberated. The eventual death throes of the Third Reich would be felt with devastating defeats at the Battle of the Bulge and Battle of Berlin. The European theaters would be over by the middle of August, and both Mussolini and Hitler would be dead.

In the Pacific, the war would rage on after the final surrender of the Germans in Europe. Here, the world is exposed to a new form of weapon. One so devastating that its effects are still felt today—the nuclear bomb.

Japan's final surrender would come at the beginning of September, and the devastation of WWII would be ended. When all was said and done, over 60 million people had died.

Concentration Camps Liberated

One of the most heinous parts of the Nazi agenda was the construction of concentration camps that would end up being death camps for millions of Jews and other non-conforming people of Europe. These camps not only used these individuals as slave labor of many Nazi construction projects but were explicitly built to eradicate any opposition to the Nazi agenda. They were known about by many but had no idea of the slaughters committed within their barbed wire fences.

Starting in 1945, the truth of what was going on within their walls became very evident as Allied forces began to liberate camp after camp. Places like Ravensbrück, Auschwitz, Bergen-Belsen, and Dachau all liberated, and the remaining inhabitants freed.

The year started with the liberation of the camp that would become what most think of when thinking of the Holocaust's atrocities—Auschwitz. The Russians had been pushing further and further into the west, driving the

Germans back from the annexed and occupied nations of Belarus and Poland. But what the Soviet Army would roll into when they entered the area surrounding the Polish town of Oswiecim would shock even the Russians.

They had been introduced to the viciousness of the Germans in both Stalingrad and Leningrad. As the Russians neared the camp, the Germans knew they had to protect themselves and began evacuation processes: setting the healthy prisoners on a march and cramming others into railway cars and shipping them off to concentration camps within the German borders. Those that were not healthy enough or close to death were left behind.

After the prisoners were removed from the camp, the remaining German forces set about destroying the evidence, knowing that if the real horrors became known to the world, the Allied forces would push harder, and there may be more dire consequences if they were defeated. These soldiers would explode and burn down houses as well as the crematoriums.

By the time late January rolled around, the primary cover-up had been completed, and the SS officers had left, abandoning the remaining prisoners to their own devices.

They had left no food, no water, nor any fuel to heat the buildings. The remaining prisoners used piles of clothes and anything they could burn to try and stay warm, and those that were healthier spent their time tending to the sicker.

The Russian troops had no idea that Auschwitz or Birkenau even existed, so when they stumbled upon the camp, they were shocked. Though not a part of their orders, the Russian commander and troops knew that something had to be done. The scout sent word to the main body of the units, and the troops were soon walking through the camp, taking in the inhumane living conditions the prisoners had been left in.

The soldiers began to set up hospitals and enlisted the help of the people living around the camp. Months after the liberation, Red Cross workers were still fighting to save the lives of thousands of prisoners with minimal supplies. Of the approximately 9,000 prisoners that had been abandoned in the camp, 7,500 survived.

Camp after camp was discovered and liberated, including the very first-ever built, Dachau. Located in southern Germany near Munich, this had been the prototype for the concentration camp system built and headed by SS Commander Heinrich Himmler.

Just one month after Hitler took power, the camp did not see the same types of atrocities committed within its walls. This camp, like others, was primarily a labor camp. The prisoners of Dachau helped build the camp itself as well as with armament production. The camp was also a training center for the SS guards that would be sent to other camps like Auschwitz. Though they had a crematorium and gas chamber, they were not used as frequently as in other camps; instead, the prisoners were subjected to medical experiments. Within the fencing of this camp, prisoners were subjected to experiments like changes in atmospheric pressure along with tests to find vaccines for malaria and tuberculosis—which they would be infected with.

The Germans began to run out of places to run. As the Allied forces marched further into the country, it became evident that they would have to move their camp prisoners deeper into the country to keep the Allies from really learning what had been going on. In April, it became evident that Dachau would be taken by U.S. soldiers soon.

The Germans had an even bigger problem. Dachau was one of the camps that had taken prisoners from other camps at the beginning of the year. With this influx of people, the camp started to fall apart. Not only were the conditions in the barracks more horrible than they had ever been, but there was also a severe Typhus epidemic. When it became evident that the camp was going to fall, the SS leaders, like they did in Auschwitz, marched the healthier prisoners south to Tegernsee. After they sent the prisoners on their death march, the rest of the guards abandoned the camp.

Two days after the Nazis had lined up 7,000 prisoners and forced them to begin their long, and for some their final march, the 45th Infantry approach Dachau. As the troops rolled toward the camp, the soldiers spotted more than two dozen railway cars, and the scent coming from them was pungent. The troops halted to examine, and what they found scarred most of them for life.

In the railroad cars were bodies upon bodies in different stages of decomposition. The infantry, filled with anger and disgust, approached the camp. There was gunfire, but there were not enough SS guards left to make it much of a battle. After a brief battle, the soldiers of the 45th Infantry entered the camp. Inside the camp, they would find 30,000 more prisoners as well as more bodies.

In a fit of anger, the American troops, sickened by what they saw, lined up several of the SS guards they had captured and executed them. The camp was liberated, and all that was left was to get help for the prisoners and bury the dead.

As the months progressed, more and more camps would fall. Some would surrender like Bergen-Belsen, and others would put up a fight. Still, in the end, the Allied forces were able to liberate every last one of the camps and free thousands of prisoners that had been subjected to unimaginable trauma, the likes of which had never been seen before.

The Holocaust would leave thousands with no home to go to, which would eventually lead to the creation of Israel as an independent state.

The German Government would also be appalled by their part in the horrors committed and began to make reparations to individuals as well as the Jewish people.

Yalta Conference

As it began to look like more and more of the Allied forces were going to be victorious, the three countries that had the most stake in the war met once again to discuss what Europe and the world would look like post-WWII.

In February of 1945, Roosevelt, Churchill, and Stalin all agreed to meet up at the Black Sea resort town of Yalta. France had been liberated as well as Belgium, and the Allied forces and the Russian Army were closing in on German borders.

Going into this meeting, the Soviet leader was able to levy his victories in Poland, Bulgaria, and Romania to give himself a bargaining advantage when it came to many of the topics to be discussed.

Though there were a lot of gains in Europe and the battle was sure to be over within the next few months, Roosevelt knew that the Pacific Theater would take a little longer to win. One of the big agendas on his plate was to make sure that Stalin would agree to send his forces to the aid of the U.S. forces that were fighting the Japanese forces in Asia and the islands.

The Russians had a history with the Japanese. Stalin had no problem promising that once Germany surrendered that Russian troops would be redirected to the western borders of Russia. This troop movement would take a few months but would be done quickly.

However, Stalin wasn't going to put his men in danger for no gain. For him to send his troops to support the Americans, he would want some guarantees from Roosevelt. He wanted the U.S. to recognize the Mongolian people's republic as its own sovereign nation as well as allow Russia to regain control of lands lost during the Russo-Japanese War.

Another concern was how the Allied forces were going to ensure that Germany would not be able to do what they had done in both WWI and WWII. The final decision was that Germany would be divided up into four zones, each controlled by one of the four leading global powers—the U.S., Britain, France, and Russia.

The city of Berlin would also be divided up in the same way. Though France was not in attendance, Stalin agreed to this as long as the zone allocated to the French would be taken from the British and American divisions. It was also decided that there should be a demilitarization as well as a denazification of Germany.

Germany would need to make reparations for all the destruction the Reich had cost.

Eastern Europe was also a point of contention as many of the nations were recently liberated and would be looking to form new governments and trying to rebuild. Then there was Poland. Stalin was reasonably open when it came to places like Bulgaria, Romania, and Czechoslovakia, but Poland, there was no give in his stance.

Poland had seen how Germany had penetrated Russia's borders the last two wars, and because of this, Stalin was not willing to relinquish the Polish territory he had taken in 1939. He would also not negotiate with the Polish Government in exile in England. Stalin was willing to allow other parties to participate in the government and to guarantee that the elections in Poland would be sanction-free elections. The Soviet Union would back free elections and the rest of the Eastern European nations as well.

Roosevelt and Churchill had already agreed to the formation and their participation in the United Nations at the

Atlantic Conference, but Stalin would pledge his involvement in the Yalta Conference.

Russia, along with the U.S. and Britain, would be permanent members of the organization and would hold the power of veto when issues and bills were brought before the organization.

Once the conference was complete, the three leaders agreed that once the surrender of Germany was finalized, they would meet again to finalize everything.

Final Battles

The final year of the war would bring some of the most iconic and bloody battles. The Germans and the Japanese could feel the noose tightening but did not want to admit the war was lost. This feeling would bring them to try new tactics and fight to their dying breaths. Opening the year, you would have on the Western front the Battle of the Bulge, and then closing out the war, the tactical genius of the Battle of Berlin.

In the Pacific, you would have not only the Battle of Iwo Jima but also the Battle of Okinawa. These battles would cement the Allies assured victory and cost both sides thousands of lives.

Hitler knew that things were getting dire at the end of 1944, and that is why he crafted a plan that would have the Allied forces fighting in the severe winter temperatures and the fatigue of fighting incessantly for years.

Along with his military commanders, Hitler derived a plan that was intended to split the Allied forces into individual forces as they drove toward the borders of Germany. By doing this, he felt that they would be able to pick off the troops one by one. The battle began in early December of '44 and would continue for six grueling and devastating weeks. The Battle of Ardennes would pair 30 German divisions against several Americans as they battled through 85 miles of thick forest.

The Germans would use every tactic possible to ensure victory, including sending double agents into the midst of the American troops. These imposters would spread false information, and some even would change road signs to keep the U.S. forces confused. The battle would wage on, coming to a head at the Belgium city of Bastogne. After the 101st parachuted into the town, they were surrounded and needed help.

In late December, Patton pushed through and rescued the 101st, and a month later, the Allies were able to beat the Germans back and claim a victory. Once that was done, they turned their sights to Berlin. The Battle of the Bulge would end up going down in the history books as the bloodiest and most costly battle that the U.S. military had ever taken part of up to that moment in history.

In the Pacific, things were starting to turn too. The Japanese Air Force and fleets had been devastated with the previous years' battles, and this left them unable to adequately protect the islands that they had occupied, including the Marshall archipelago. Armed with this intel, the U.S. military commanders felt that because of this, places like Iwo Jima would be an easy win.

Though on paper that seemed right, in actual execution, the U.S. forces would find out that storming the beaches of Iwo Jima would be much more difficult. Not only because of the environmental issues like the sand on the beach but also because the general leading the Japanese forces had instituted a new defensive tactic. Using the natural landscape and foliage of the island, the general had instructed his troops to begin building artillery positions that would be camouflaged from bombing attacks and invasions.

That defensive strategy worked as the Americans had bombed the island and then began landing Marines on the island. However, the landing became troublesome as the ashy, soft sand made maneuvering their vehicles and men on the beach supremely difficult. Lying in the brush line, though, were Japanese troops that patiently waited for the first phase to be executed—the artillery—before they charged the Marines on the beach. The Marines were able to fend off these attacks and continued landing marines for the next few days on the shores of Iwo Jima.

The battle would carry on for another five weeks before, with one final hail Mary, the Japanese bonsai attacked the U.S. troops with just 300 men. This conflict on March 25th would be the one that allowed the U.S. to claim the island as theirs—although it would be another several weeks before they had rounded up almost all of the Japanese troops. (The final two Japanese soldiers would hide on the island until 1949.)

The taking of Iwo Jima ended up not being as strategic as the military thought it would be. However, it was still a costly victory and one that because of the image taken when Mount Suribachi was taken is perhaps one of the most iconic and well-known battles of the entire war.

Berlin had been bombed, but there had never been a successful attack until April of 1945. The Soviet Army had run its way through Poland, driving the Germans out of the country. Once that was done, they set their sights on the capital city of Berlin. The Soviets would assign this task to three units—two Belarusian and one Ukrainian. The three divisions would approach the town from the east, north, and south, eventually surrounding the city, leaving the forces within it nowhere to hide.

Lieutenant General Helmuth Reymann led the Nazi forces within the city, and though it looked like they were up to the challenge, in reality, they were severely depleted and filled with aged military vets and Hitler youth. This lack of proper human resources would eventually lead to the end of the war and unconditional surrender of the Reich on May 7th, 1945.

The losses in the battle would be over 100,000 on each side, among those was the Fuhrer himself.

During the campaign, Hitler had taken his own life—see Death of Dictators (p. 136)—along with his new bride, Eva Braun.

After moving their troops into place, the three divisions of Soviet forces began the final assault on April 16th. As the soldiers started to gain ground, Hitler found little faith in the leadership of Reymann, and he replaced him with General Helmuth Weidling.

One by one, the Soviet forces began to push further into Berlin, fending off attacks from several divisions of the German troops. Finally, the Soviet troops reached the heart of Berlin and began to occupy any location that could be used as a transportation hub—the S-Bahn Railroad Station and Tempelhof Airport were some of the first.

On April 29th, the Soviets crossed the Moltke Bridge into the heart of the Interior Ministry. They took the Gestapo building first and then marched on the Reichstag.

It took a few days to make it to this area of the city. Eventually, the Soviet forces kept pushing the remaining

German soldiers back until the Chief of the General Staff, General Hans Krebs, had no other option but to enter into talks with Chuikov. While negotiating with the Russians, the Germans attempted to escape, but only a handful made it out of Berlin and into the waiting arms of the American troops.

On May 2nd, the Reich Chancellery fell, and Weidling had no other choice but to surrender. With the signing of the unconditional surrender, the European front came to an end.

Though the battle in the West was done, Japan fought on. Eventually, the U.S. forces would make their way closer and closer to the Japanese mainland, knowing that the only way to ensure victory was to attack the enemy on their home field. The right way to do this was Okinawa Island. With that knowledge, the U.S. commanders designed the plan, code-named Operation Iceberg.

Okinawa would be the entry point for the U.S., and the Japanese knew it. This lush hilly island became the home of Japanese High Command and the place where they would either be victorious or die with honor. The Americans not only knew that this was the perfect jumping-off point for an invasion of Japan, but also the capturing of the airbase on the island would cripple their enemy.

While their families back home were preparing for Easter services and celebrations, the soldiers of the 5th Fleet launched their attack. The airplanes flew over the beautiful green island and bombarded the shores and interior with bomb after bomb. Once the air raid was over, the soldiers then hopped on boats and mounted a beach landing.

Assuming that they would be met with large numbers of Japanese defense soldiers, the brass had prepared their troops for their D-Day. The pushback was not there, though, and the U.S. forces pushed passed the beachheads into the interior with little to no resistance. The American troops and command were on edge, waiting for the Japanese to attack. The Japanese commander, Lieutenant General Mitsuru Ushijima, and his 32nd Army Division lay in wait at a strategic vantage point along Shuri. He had set up his men to form a triangle defense position that would later be called the Shuri Defense Line.

The high, rugged walls of the Shuri Line made the conflict difficult but not impossible. The U.S. military forces moved as fast as they could, and though the Japanese felt they had the upper hand, made quick work of the Shuri Line, but this was not the only defense the Japanese had set up. As the Americans cleared the encampment one by one, the weather began to turn, and the hills and roads of the island became overrun with water. Flooding and muddy paths made it easier for the Japanese to get a jump at many locations. Eventually, the U.S. forces were able to make their way to Shuri castle in May and began the final push to take Okinawa. While the ground soldiers continued to fight, the fleet was not left to wait for them.

On April 7th, the Japanese battleship Yamato was deployed to attack the 5th Fleet and then help the Japanese on the island to finish the ground troops. However, submarines spotted the ship, and the fleet cut them off at the pass, sinking the ship and its crew to the bottom of the Pacific.

As the American forces moved closer to the final Japanese stronghold, the soldiers and civilians of the island felt they had only two choices—surrender or suicide. Trying to mitigate what they had already seen, General Buckner tried to encourage surrender by using propaganda dropped from the fleet ships that said the war was all but lost. This tactic, however, had the opposite effect, and hundreds of Japanese took their own lives. Eventually, 7,000 soldiers would surrender.

Instead of returning home disgraced, the general and his chief of staff decided to take their own lives, which ended the conflict and gave the U.S. their foothold to begin the invasion of Japan.

Although the new president, Harry S. Truman, would opt for a more devastating option and one that would eventually end the war in the Pacific.

Death of Dictators

It was clear that by April of 1945, the Nazi-controlled government was on its way to defeat in Northern Italy. Milan, which was made the seat of the Social Republic of Italy and headed by the escaped Mussolini, was crumbling, and even Mussolini was considering surrender.

He met with partisans to discuss this as well as other options that may keep him and his ideologies in power. Still, Mussolini soon learned that the Nazis had begun their talks with the Allies for unconditional surrender. Feeling that if that happened, it wouldn't be long before he was in the custody of Allied forces once again, Mussolini fled with his girlfriend for the city.

Unfortunately, as he tried to escape, his celebrity betrayed him, and they were captured near the town of Dongo. Fearing another attempt by the remaining Nazi forces to rescue the dictator, his captors hid him away in a farmhouse.

Early the next morning, Mussolini and his girlfriend were forced into a vehicle and driven to Giulino di Mezzegra on the shores of Lake Como. Dragged from the car, they were told to stand in front of a wall. The partisans then stood before them with machine guns, and in a flurry of bullets, the dictator and his lover were executed. The corpses were tossed in a truck with a dozen other fascists' corpses and dumped in the center of Piazzale Loreto in Milan.

Mussolini's body was left out in the open, and the citizens of the city began throwing things at it, beating it, even shooting it. Eventually, the bodies of several dead fascists—including Mussolini—were tied and suspended for all to see within the square. American troops would later remove the body and transport it to the morgue. With the death of Il Duce, the fascist period in Italian history was over, as was their participation in the war.

Hitler had been hidden away in his secret bunker for months to protect him from any further attempts on his life. The shelter was like a small home, and he had made sure everything he loved was in it. He had even gotten married there, but as the Russian forces grew closer, it became evident to him and his closest confidants that there may come a need for a backup plan.

Many of his inner circle pleaded with him to escape and make his way to the Eagle's Nest, his home in Bavaria. But he refused, and he and his trusted confidants decided that if it needed to be done, suicide would be the only way to ensure they weren't arrested.

His officers entered the meeting rooms on April 30th and informed him that the Russians had taken the chancellery. It was only a matter of time before they found the bunker below it. So Hitler and his new bride, Eva Braun, swallowed a cyanide pill. Hitler was afraid the pill would not work and shot himself with a pistol.

Hitler had left explicit orders for his body to be cremated after he had seen what the crowds had done to Mussolini. The remaining bunker inhabitants honored his wishes and burned his body and Eva's body in the garden of the chancellery.

Conclusion

The taking of Berlin and the death of Hitler marked the end of the war. A war that had waged for seven years and cost millions of lives would be the defining factor in many problems to come.

Its destruction would be felt for decades to come, and some of the charters and decisions made at its end would ripple through the world, setting the stage for conflicts and future wars. The devastation would leave vast sections of land in Europe and Asia.

There would be new countries emerging and new ideologies taking a deeper hold in parts of the world. Over the seven years, approximately four percent of the world had been killed. New precedents in law would be set, and a destructive new weapon would come to light.

On May 7th, at Reims, the Germans signed the unconditional surrender. Though the Japanese had not yet surrendered, the Allied forces and the Soviet Union believed the war was over, and that meant it was time to reconvene the leaders and make the final decisions on some significant factors. This gathering would occur in Potsdam, a city outside of Berlin.

The new U.S. President Truman would meet with Churchill and Stalin and lay out a plan for what was to happen in Germany as well as the Eastern-Bloc. The Pacific was not forgotten in the conference as the three leaders agreed that a declaration of unconditional surrender should be sent to the Japanese Government—they also decided that the Emperor should remain in power once that surrender had occurred.

When the meeting was finished, the lines were drawn for what post-war Europe would look like, which would lead to decades of mistrust between the western world and the communist nations housed behind the Iron curtain.

The U.S. and the USSR would eventually become rivals, and the cold war would begin.

With Germany taken care of, the Japanese were the only Axis power still left. Though they had received the declaration of unconditional surrender, it would take something much more significant to convince the Japanese Government and the Emperor that the war was over.

The U.S. had been testing a secret weapon, one that would devastate thousands of miles and leave a lasting effect on the land where it was used.

The weapon was a nuclear bomb, and the use of it was a controversial choice for Truman to make. Most of the generals were in favor of traditional bombing and then landed invasions. But this type of tactic would cost the U.S. military a significant amount of lives and money, and Truman wanted to avoid this. He turned to this new weapon, and on August 6th, the first of the two nuclear bombs was dropped on Hiroshima, Japan.

Three days later, Nagasaki would feel the same devastation. With massive destruction and casualties on August 15th, Japan had no choice but to surrender. The war in the Pacific was very strong, but at what cost? The revealing of this new devastating weapon would set the world on an original path, and the arms race for nuclear dominance would begin.

There were still a lot of things that had to be taken care of in Europe to wrap up the atrocities and devastation caused by WWII and the Third Reich. In November of 1945, after several months of deliberation and crafting of a new international military law, the Nuremberg trials would begin.

These court hearings would see the high-level Nazi leadership and civilian conspirators stand trial for the atrocities of not only the war itself but also the systematic genocide of millions of Jews.

These trials would continue for four years, with serval of the defendants being convicted and put to death. Those that didn't receive the death penalty were given prison sentences ranging from ten years to life.

The war would make the Allies into occupiers as military bases were set up in Germany and Japan to control and maintain the fragile peace that had been created by the unconditional surrendering for the two Axis powers. Factories that had once made armaments were destroyed and nations were given their sovereignty back.

The occupation of Allied forces and mandates set out by the United Nations would cause tension between communist East Germany and democratic West Germany. In the end, the two nations would divide into their entities. This division would separate families and lead to even more atrocities and conflicts.

In 1991, the Berlin wall would fall, and the two nations would have no borders anymore. The Allied plans for the Korean peninsula would also stir up some tension and, in 1950, would play a significant role in the beginnings of the Korean War.

With millions of Jews with no home to go to, the UN also created the Partition Plan, defining the borders of the Israeli state, which would set the Middle East up for decades of conflict.

The Nazi plan had destroyed Germany and left the world changed forever.

Trivia Questions & Answers

History Student

At the end of the war, the U.S. bombed Japan with two large atomic bombs. What cities were targeted?

Answer: There were many cities chosen as potential targets for the bombs. In the end, Hiroshima and Kokura were chosen. Hiroshima was home to the 2nd Army responsible for protecting South Japan, and by eliminating them, it would make it easy to invade Japan as needed. As for Nagasaki, the second bombing site was on the list of chosen points as it was an important port city. However, it was not the original target and was only selected as a backup as Kokura had been covered with heavy cloud cover.

Each of the bombs that were dropped on the two sites were given code names. What were they?

Answer: The bomb that dropped on Hiroshima was called Little Boy, and the one for Nagasaki was dubbed Fat Boy.

What were the names of the planes that dropped the atomic bombs on Japan?

Answer: The plane that dropped Little Boy was called the Enola Gay. Bockscar was the name of the aircraft that dropped Fat Boy.

After the failed Beer Hall Putsch in 1924, Hitler was arrested and sent to jail. During his time in prison, he began working on a book, what was it called?

Answer: In jail, he was convinced by his assistant, Rudolf Hess, to write down his thoughts and ideologies so that he could deliver them to more people. What came from this encouragement was the book, *Mein Kampf* (My Struggles).

In 1944, the Allied forces stormed the beaches of Normandy in an effort to liberate France. What was the code name given this operation?

Answer: The storming of the beaches of Normandy took a lot of preparation, and the entire operation was code-named Overlord. On June 6th, the action was launched, and within a few weeks, Northern France was liberated from Nazi occupation.

What U.S. Armed Service was not its own entity until after WWII?

Answer: After the war, the Army Air Corps would split from the main force to form its own service—the Air Force. Though many bases across the globe still house both services, they still work very closely.

From WWI, the global community got the League of Nations as a peace and security organization. But what peace and security organization came from WWII and is still part of the global government?

Answer: After the League of Nations collapsed after WWI, the world leaders knew there needed to be a global governing entity, but it wasn't until the end of WWII that they crafted the charter that would give the world the United Nations.

Breaking the codes that the Germans were sending from unit to unit was crucial to being able to defeat the Third Reich. Who helped crack the Enigma code?

Answer: The Enigma code had been deciphered before, but before the war broke out, the Germans had changed the ciphering system. Mathematician Alan Turing and another code breaker, Gordon Welchman, devoted their time to deciphering the code, and while doing this, created a machine known as the Bombe. This device was used by code breakers to reduce the work needed to translate the code messages sent by the Nazis.

The Battle of Britain was one of the first major battles fought in the war. What did Hitler name the plan to be executed against England?

Answer: Hitler knew he would have to take out the British before he could even start with the Russians, so he and his military leaders crafted a plan and dubbed it Operation Sea Lion.

How did the Battle of Britain get its name?

Answer: The battle got its name before the conflict had even started. Winston Churchill had delivered his famous "Finest Hour" speech, and within it had said that the battle for France was over. He followed this statement by saying that he expected the Battle of Britain would be the next.

In 1935, a set of laws were passed that paved the way for the atrocities of the Holocaust. What were these laws called?

Answer: In 1935, two separate laws made it through the Reichstag—the Reich Citizenship Law and the Law for the Protection of German Blood and German Honor. These laws would strip Jewish citizens of their German citizenship and dictated how an individual could be defined as a Jew. The second law banned marriage and sexual relations between a German citizen and an individual of Jewish descent. These two laws would come to be known as the Nuremberg Laws.

Having inspired Hitler's attempt to overthrow the government, who was the leader of the coup in Italy?

Answer: The fascist leader of the revolutionaries in Italy was Il Duce, otherwise known as the dictator Benito Mussolini.

After the Beer Hall Putsch, Hitler was arrested, tried, and found guilty of the charges. How long was he sentenced for?

Answer: Though some would argue that the way Hitler spent his sentence was not really a prison sentence, he still served five months in jail before getting out to reclaim his place in the Nazi Party.

The Germans had been forced to sign the Treaty of Versailles, and from the moment that they did, some entities began defying the stipulations within its pages. What was the first visible defiance of the treaty?

Answer: On March 7th, 1936, Hitler, after declaring that the German nations would not abide by the rules and regulations of the Treaty of Versailles, rolled his troops into the demilitarized zone in the Rhineland.

Though the main concentration targets were the Jewish community, other groups were targeted as being non-German. What were some of these groups?

Answer: The Holocaust was a horrific event in history, but along with the millions of Jews that lost their lives, there were gypsies, gays, communists, the mentally ill, the handicapped, and religious leaders that were targeted as well.

Five months after taking power, Hitler and his inner circle began building concentration camps. What was the first one to open its gates?

Answer: The first camp and the template for all other camps was the one opened in a small town on the outskirts of Munich, Dachau. The camp opened on March 22nd, 1933.

Besides being the first concentration camp, what else was Dachau known for?

Answer: Dachau would turn into the training post for all SS soldiers that were set to be stationed at concentration camps. It was also the first camp to use its inmates as test subjects in some cruel medical experiments.

The death toll at many of the liberated concentration camps may never be truly known. The most well-known camp is, of course, Auschwitz. How many people are estimated to have died at this camp?

Answer: It is estimated that somewhere between one and one and a half million people were killed in Auschwitz. The vast majority of them were of the Jewish community, but gypsy and Polish dissidents were also among the victims.

In 1945, many of the concentration camps were liberated. One of the first was Auschwitz. What country's soldiers liberated this camp?

Answer: Having continued their push to remove the Germans from occupied lands in Eastern Europe, Russian soldiers stumbled upon the camp, and when they saw the emaciated prisoners living in filth, they quickly began setting up medical treatment faculties.

About a week before the unconditional surrender, the first-ever concentration camp fell. Who liberated Dachau?

Answer: On April 29th, after a few resistance battles, the 45th Infantry Division of the U.S. 7th Army entered the gates of Dachau to an unnerving discovery. The troops had heard stories of other liberations, but when seeing it with their own eyes, it was more horrific than they had expected.

The death toll at each concentration camp was tragic. How many people are estimated to have died at Dachau?

Answer: When the records were examined and bodies exhumed, the number of people that died at Dachau is estimated to be approximately 32,000.

The defensive border on the French front ran from Switzerland to the English Channel. What was this line called?

Answer: The French defensive line was called the Maginot Line.

The Germans plowed through the lowlands and through Northern France on their way to take Paris. When did Germany enter Paris?

Answer: The fight was hard, but Hitler and the Reich wanted to take Paris to have control of the coast. On June 14th, 1940, German troops entered the city for the first time.

At the beginning of the war, who was the Russian Foreign Minister?

Answer: Responsible for things like the Molotov-Ribbentrop Pact, the Russian Foreign Minister at the beginning of WWII was Vyacheslav Molotov.

Hitler had always intended to attack Russia. But he had a few things he had to take care of first, but by the summer of 1941, they had been done. When did Hitler march on to Russia?

Answer: On June 22nd, 150 divisions and 300 tanks marched for 2,000 miles from the North Cape to the Black Sea.

What was the Atlantic Charter?

Answer: The Atlantic Charter was the document created by Roosevelt and Churchill at the Atlantic Conference. This meeting was made to discuss what the world would look like post-war once the Allied forces had won.

What global organization did it help to build after the war?

Answer: Within several days of meetings, an outline of the ideas and rules that would help make the world safer was created, and these would later become the tenets of the United Nations.

Once the Atlantic Charter was shared with the world, how many nations would sign it initially?

Answer: The initial charter was signed by 26 nations of the world, including the U.S., Britain, China, and France.

Germany began its expansion before it invaded Poland. What was the first country that was annexed by the Reich?

Answer: The first country that joined the Reich was Austria. On March 13rd, 1941, Hitler entered his homeland to the cheers of an adoring crowd and, with no bloodshed, took over Austria.

Before Germany could start its run for dominance, it made several pacts. One of them was with Italy. What was this pact named?

Answer: The pact between Italy and Germans was known as the Pact of Steel or the Pact of Friendship and Alliance.

What was the Sudetenland?

Answer: The Sudetenland was a strip of land that belonged to Czechoslovakia, comprised of the Bohemian and Moravian sections of the country. The Germans wanted this strip of land because it held a large population of German citizens that had been separated from their homeland by the Treaty of Versailles.

The Japanese attack on Pearl Harbor was instigated by several economic sanctions placed on Japan. Why did the U.S. place embargoes on Japan?

Answer: The Japanese had been expanding their empire, and the biggest target on their radar was China. They had led several massive invasions, and each of them was more viscous than the next. With their attack on Nanking, known as the rape of Nanking, the atrocities became too much for the U.S. Government. In retaliation for their horrific massacre, the U.S. placed embargoes on fuel and many other goods.

With the embargoes placed on their goods, the Japanese wanted to strike back. After making moves on several islands in the Philippine Sea, the Japanese Naval Command set their sights on the naval base at Pearl Harbor. How many miles did the Japanese fleet have to travel to get there?

Answer: The Japanese fleet would have to travel 4,000 miles to get positioned for their attack on Peral Harbor.

The attack on Pearl Harbor is perhaps one of the most infamous assaults on U.S. soil. What time did the strike begin?

Answer: The attack would officially begin at eight in the morning on Sunday, December 7th, 1941.

The siege of Leningrad was one of the longest-running sieges in history. How long did the attack last?

Answer: Though the siege is often referred to as the 900-day siege, the blockade actually only lasted 872 days.

What injuries did Hitler experience from the bomb planted in the Wolf's Lair?

Answer: Hitler was one of the only people that survived the attack. He came out of it with severe burns over his body, a busted eardrum, and one arm temporarily paralyzed.

Eisenhower had considered delaying the liberation of Paris, but the French General Charles De Gaulle convinced Eisenhower to reconsider. How did he do this?

Answer: De Gaulle assured Eisenhower that if they struck, his intelligence said they would experience very little resistance. Then there was the fact that if they waited, the communist resistance might end up liberating Paris, and that would throw the post-war government of France into turmoil.

What was the first city liberated in the Minsk Offensive?

Answer: The first city liberated from German occupation was the Belarusian city of Borisov.

When did the Battle of the Philippine Sea begin?

Answer: The Pacific Theater was full of epic battles, but the Battle of the Philippine Sea may well be one of the most epic, but short. The battle began on June 19th, 1944.

When did the Battle of the Leyte Gulf take place?

Answer: The battle started October 20th and raged on for five days, concluding October 25th.

At the end of the war, the three major leaders gathered together again in Yalta. What was the Yalta Conference about?

Answer: This conference was between Roosevelt, Churchill, and Stalin and was a meeting about what would happen after the war. They decided what would happen to Germany after the war as well as the rest of Europe, Russia's entrance into the Pacific Theater, and the creation of the United Nations.

Why was Poland such a considerable part of the negotiations for Stalin at the Yalta Conference?

Answer: The past two wars had seen the Germans use Poland as an entry point, not Russian borders. He wanted to ensure that this would never be the case again.

What was Hitler's objective at the Battle of the Bulge?

Answer: He aimed to drive a wedge between the Allied forces, breaking them into separate units as the drive to obtain Berlin. This would weaken them and allow his depleted forces to have a better chance of victory.

How many weeks did the Battle of the Bulge last?

Answer: The battle began in mid-December and went through to late January of the following year. In total, the battle lasted six weeks.

What U.S. military division defended Bastogne?

Answer: The 101st Airborne Division defended the city of Bastogne.

Who was the commander of the 101st Airborne Division at Bastogne?

Answer: The man in charge was General Anthony McAuliffe.

What day did the iconic image of the taking of Mount Suribachi take place?

Answer: The photographer Joe Rosenthal captured the image on February 23rd, 1945.

When did the Battle of Iwo Jima end?

Answer: The remaining Japanese forces mounted a 300-man Banzai attack that failed to gain any traction, and soon there was no path to winning for the Japanese. On March 25th, the Allied forces claimed victory.

After the victory at Iwo Jima, what was the island used for?

Answer: There was no significant tactical advantage to the island when it came down to it. The Seabees were sent to rebuild the airfields, and the island became an emergency landing place for U.S. Air Forces.

When does the Battle of Berlin come to its conclusion?

Answer: The Battle of Berlin was deemed a victory on May 2nd, at six in the morning.

Many things occurred due to the Russian victory at the Battle of Berlin. What were some of the consequences of the battle?

Answer: Amidst the gunfire and bombing of the battle, Hitler committed suicide, and with that, Donitz became president. The war in Europe came to an end, and five days after the end of the battle, Germany signed an unconditional surrender.

What spurred Hitler to commit suicide?

Answer: The Russians had moved into Berlin and had taken the chancellery. The bunker he was living in was under the building, and it would eventually be discovered.

How did Hitler kill himself?

Answer: Hitler and his new bride took cyanide pills. Afraid that the pills would not be enough to kill him, Hitler also took his service pistol and shot himself.

How long did the Battle of Okinawa last?

Answer: The initial battle began on Easter Sunday of 1945. The battle would wage on for over two months, finally coming to its conclusion on June 22nd.

What battleship was sent by the Japanese to attack the 5th Fleet during the Battle for Okinawa?

Answer: The Japanese Naval Command sent the battleship Yamato to engage with the 5th Fleet.

Mussolini was put into power after the Nazis rescued him from imprisonment in the Social Republic of Italy. This puppet state was governed out of what Italian city?

Answer: The Social Republic of Italy was led from the northern Italian city of Milan.

What caused Mussolini to flee from Milan?

Answer: He was informed that the Nazis had begun talks for an unconditional surrender. This would mean that his support would be depleted, and he would soon be the next one on the Allied hit list.

How was Mussolini executed?

Answer: Mussolini and his mistress were caught trying to flee Milan and were taken to a small village near Lake Como. They were told to stand in front of a wall and were executed by firing squad.

What happened to Mussolini's corpse after his execution?

Answer: The people who had executed him took his body and his mistress' body and dumped them in the center of Piazzale Loreto. The people who had lived under his fascist regime took their anger out on his corpse. They kicked it, spit on it, and shot it. Then the body was tied by the feet and suspended from a building in the square.

When did Germany and Japan surrender?

Answer: Germany was the first to surrender. On May 7th, 1945, the German leadership signed its unconditional surrender. The Japanese would take a few more months. On August 14th, 1945, the Japanese would declare their submission, but it wouldn't be for another couple of weeks on September 2nd that the final surrender was signed.

When was the Potsdam Conference convened?

Answer: The conference took place between July 17th and August 2nd, 1945.

What was discussed at the Potsdam Conference?

Answer: It was the last of the WWII meetings with the "Big Three" heads of state: U.S. President Truman, British Prime Minister Churchill, and Soviet Premier Stalin. They discussed the German economy, the punishment for war criminals, land boundaries, and reparations.

How many years did the Nuremberg trials last?

Answer: The trials would take four years to be completed. They would last from 1945 to 1949.

What was the main difficulty of getting the trials underway?

Answer: No trials like these had ever been done, so there was no precedent for what the United Nations was trying to accomplish.

What were the three criminal categories that the tribunal came up with to charge the Nazi leadership with?

Answer: The tribunal broke the crimes down into three categories: crimes against peace, crimes against humanity, and war crimes.

Who was the prosecuting attorney at the Nuremberg trials?

Answer: Robert H. Jackson would be the chief counsel against the Nazi leaders and conspirators.

What were the consequences caused by WWII?

Answer: Several ramifications would ripple over the world for decades. Germany was divided into two nations, plans for the Korean peninsula would also help further tensions and lead to the Korean war in 1950. The Jewish population had tons of people without a home, so a new state was created in the Middle East. The creation of the new state of Israel would cause friction in the Middle East that is still felt today. Tensions between the Russians and Americans would escalate, and decades of espionage known as the Cold War would ensue. The use of nuclear bombs in Japan would also ignite an arms race.

History Buff

What was the plan for the massive land invasion of Japan called?

Answer: The land invasion of Japan was to be called Operation Downfall. However, because Truman opted to use nuclear bombs, the plan was never executed.

What was the site of the signing of Japan's unconditional surrender?

Answer: The site chosen was the USS Missouri. The ship had seen a lot of action, but it didn't have as decorated a commission as the other ships in the fleet. The vessel was chosen simply because it was the flagship of the 3rd Fleet, and for appearances, it made sense to use the flagship as the site for such an auspicious occasion.

Coded messages were essential tactics used in the war. What was the Native American language used by the U.S. Marines?

Answer: The U.S. Marines enlisted soldiers from the Navajo Nation and used their own unique language to code messages. The use of this language proved impossible for the enemies to decipher and played a significant role in the U.S. success in the war.

When Hitler gave Erwin Rommel control of the Northern European front, he was charged with completing the Atlantic Wall. What was the Atlantic Wall?

Answer: The Atlantic Wall was a defensive line that ran 2,499 miles down the Atlantic coast of Europe. This defensive line contained bunkers, minefields, and obstacles both on land as well as in the water. These were all in place to help keep the Allied forces from attacking via the English Channel.

As one of the many diversionary tactics, what locations did the Allied forces make the German military command think was going to be the site of their great invasion?

Answer: Using false communications and double agents, the Allied forces chose a few probable targets. Some of these included Norway as well as the Pas-de-Calais.

A Scottish physicist, Robert Watson-Watt, invented a radio wave-based weapon, but that weapon became another helpful tool for the Allies. What did that weapon become?

Answer: The tool that could use radio waves to locate an enemy became a tactical advantage for land, air, and sea battles. This invention would come to be known as the radar.

Kamikaze pilots were a vital tactic used by the Japanese during the Pacific Theater. In total, how many crashed their planes during the war?

Answer: Approximately 2,800 planes and their crew were sent out on suicide missions called Kamikaze missions.

With approximately 2,800 Kamikaze missions during the war, how much damage was inflicted on the Allied forces?

Answer: Those missions delivered significant damages to the Allied forces, where 4,900 sailors lost their lives, and approximately 34 ships were lost.

The U.S. began to shun anything that was of German descent or origin. With that being said, two foods got new names because of this. What two foods had a rebranding during the war?

Answer: The hamburger and sauerkraut got a new name and a different image. To give them a more patriotic flair and to remove any German affiliation, the hamburger became the

Liberty steak, and sauerkraut became Liberty cabbage. The names didn't stick, though!

Who was the leader of the Royal Air Force when the Battle of Britain began?

Answer: In the First World War, the head of the RAF Air Field, Marshal Hugh Dowding, served as a pilot, and when WWII broke out, he had the distinct honor of commanding the RAF.

Why did Hitler eventually greenlight the blitz in London?

Answer: Though not a successful bombing, the RAF had attempted to strike at the political heart of Germany—Berlin. Once this had been done, Hitler felt there was no other choice but to retaliate, and he greenlit the blitz.

Before the Germans' socialist party was called the Nazi Party, it was the German Workers' Party. How did Hitler become a member of this political party?

Answer: The military had been hearing rumors of these radical meetings at beer halls and knew that they needed to get a handle on them, so they began sending spies into them. One of these was a young journalist named Adolf Hitler. He realized he really believed in what was being said at the meetings and soon joined the party.

Once the party had changed its name, they began gathering yearly for the Nazi Congress. When was the first one held?

Answer: The first Nazi Congress was held in Munich on January 23rd, 1923.

The Nazi Party could feel that Germany was ready for new leadership and decided to follow the lead of their neighbors to the south—Italy—and plan a coup. What was this coup called?

Answer: This coup was called the Beer Hall Putsch. The coup failed even with the support from WWI hero, Erich von Ludendorff. The failure would find Hitler in prison and several of the inner circle fleeing to nearby Austria.

The failed coup, known as the Beer Hall Putsch, was executed when?

Answer: The political maneuver was executed on the night of November 9th, 1923, in Munich, Germany.

Mussolini's revolutionary coup in Italy encouraged Hitler to do the same. When did Mussolini's coup take place?

Answer: Mussolini marched on Rome and was able to take power on October 30th, 1922.

When Hitler and the Nazi Party refocused and decided to take the country by political maneuverings, they had one big obstacle in their way, and that was the German president. Who was the German president in 1925?

Answer: The man sitting at the helm of the German state was none other than WWI hero Paul von Hindenburg.

In 1924, several people met in an attempt to help solve Germany's reparation problem. From this meeting came the Dawes Act. What role did this plan have to play in the rise of the Nazi Party?

Answer: The Nazi Party was unable to get the foothold they wanted because the German economy was booming, thanks to the 80 million dollars in loans taken out from U.S. companies and individuals. These loans tied the German economy to the United States, and in 1929, when the stock market crashed, so did the German economy. This crash left the Nazis with the perfect example of how relying on others undermined the German people and their honor.

Horrible medical experiments were done on prisoners in the concentration camps. One of the worst camps for this was Auschwitz. Who was the insane doctor that perpetrated these horrible crimes at Auschwitz?

Answer: At the beginning of the war, Josef Mengele was a medical officer assigned to the SS. However, in 1943, appointed by Heinrich Himmler, he would become the chief doctor at the camp, and here he would commit horrible atrocities in the name of what he called science.

Many think that Auschwitz was just one camp. In truth, the complex was made up of three specific sites, all with their own purpose. What were the three sites that made up the Auschwitz concentration camp?

Answer: Auschwitz, of course, was the main camp, and it was typically used for holding political prisoners. There was Birkenau, which was the extermination camp. Then there was Monowitz, a labor camp.

When the Auschwitz camp was evacuated, there were tons of prisoners left behind. How many prisoners were left at Auschwitz?

Answer: When the Russians liberated the camp, there were approximately 9,000 prisoners still housed in the camp.

Another camp that was liberated in the final months of the war was Bergen-Belsen. Which member of the Allied forces liberated this camp?

Answer: In April of 1945, as one of the last camps to be taken before the surrender, Bergen-Belsen was liberated by Allied forces made up of both Canadian and British troops.

When the camp of Bergen-Belsen was liberated, some of the prisoners turned on the kapo and killed them. What was a kapo?

Answer: A kapo was a prisoner chosen by the SS to supervise laborers and complete simple administrative tasks. Feeling these prisoners had betrayed their people, there was a revolt on April 15th, and 170 kapos were killed.

After the prisoners had been liberated, what happened to Bergen-Belsen?

Answer: The Typhus outbreak, coupled with lice, could not be contained, and the Allied forces rolled in with tanks and guns and burned the camp to the ground.

Dachau was known for its experiments on patients. In fact, it was the first concentration camp to do this. What kind of inhumane tests were done on prisoners at the camp?

Answer: The doctors and scientists at Dachau performed tests that included the effects of changes in atmospheric pressure on the human body, how cold affected the human body, experiments for vaccines and treatments for tuberculosis and malaria, the ability to make seawater drinkable, and ways to halt severe bleeding.

What was the Rome-Berlin Axis?

Answer: This was a treaty, signed in October of 1936, that cemented the friendship between Hitler's Nazi regime in Germany and Mussolini's Fascist one in Italy.

Once Poland had been taken and divided between Germany and Russia, what country was the next to be invaded by Germany?

Answer: Next up on the hit list were Norway and Denmark. Both of these locations would help Hitler gain control of the North Sea and give him good access points to the Atlantic. Norway was also rich in iron ore, and that would benefit the Reich greatly as the war progressed.

Like with all great military maneuvers, the plan to invade Denmark and Norway was given a code name. What was the code name?

Answer: Seeing as the campaign was intended to give the Reich control of the North Sea waterways, the code name given to the mission was Operation Weserübung. This name literally translates to water exercise.

Denmark did not give that much resistance when Hitler demanded they hand over control to the Nazis. Who was the King of Denmark at the time?

Answer: King Christian X felt that his army didn't have a chance, and to spare his soldiers' lives, he surrendered to the demands quickly.

What British Prime Minister resigned his post in May of 1940?

Answer: Neville Chamberlain had failed and been duped by Hitler that there could be peace. When Hitler blatantly declared war, Chamberlain had to resign to save face. In his place, the indomitable Winston Churchill took charge of the office and would eventually lead his country to victory—with a little help from some friends.

What was the Molotov-Ribbentrop Pact?

Answer: This was a treaty signed by both the Germans and Russians that stated there would be no aggression between the two nations. It also detailed how Poland would be divided between the two once occupied. This treaty was signed in preparation for the invasion of Poland in 1939.

Where was the Molotov-Ribbentrop Pact signed?

Answer: The pact, with a term of ten years, was signed in the halls of the Kremlin in Moscow.

In the treaty of Versailles, the German military was limited to 100,000 soldiers. But in the 1930s, Hitler began secret rearmament, and that included the building of a massive air force, the Luftwaffe. Who helped the Germans rebuild their air force?

Answer: Headed up by Hermann Goring, the Luftwaffe was built up in secret with the help of the Russians.

The Germans marched toward Moscow and Leningrad, but before they got there, they would have to take multiple cities. What were the three main Soviet cities that were taken first?

Answer: The first three cities that German forces were able to occupy were: Minsk, Smolensk, and Kyiv.

Operation Barbarossa was an ambitious campaign but would ultimately fail. What were the factors that contributed to its failure?

Answer: Several things contributed to Germany's failure. The weather was one. Spring rains made the ground muddy and delayed the German troops' progression, and then when winter came, the Germans were ill-equipped to handle the harsh temperatures. There were also civilian forces that mobilized and attacked the soldiers. The familiarity of the land also gave the advantage to Russian troops.

The two leaders needed a quiet place to meet away from the prying eyes of the media to discuss the Atlantic Charter. Where did Roosevelt and Churchill meet?

Answer: The charter would be released to the public on August 14th, 1941, but before it was finished, the two wanted a beautiful place to formulate their ideas. They chose a naval ship anchored in Placentia Bay, in Canada.

When Austria was annexed, there was no resistance, and part of that had to do with the leadership in power at the time. Who was the chancellor of Austria when Germany annexed the nation?

Answer: The chancellor in March of 1941 was Kurt von Schuschnigg.

Once the Reich annexed Austria, what happened to the chancellor?

Answer: He was forced to resign and then imprisoned until the war ended in 1945.

In January of 1942, select Nazi leaders were invited to a conference at Wannsee. What was the meeting in regards to?

Answer: The Wannsee Conference was set up so that the final decision on what was to be done with the Jewish communities of Europe will be finalized. Some of the things that would be decided were the use of extermination camps, which eventually would bring about the worst atrocity known to man—the Holocaust.

The decree that would come from the Wannsee Conference was dubbed the "Final Solution." Who was the author of this document?

Answer: The horror that would come to be known as the "Final Solution" was the idea of Reinhard Heidrich, the right-hand of Heinrich Himmler.

The Doolittle Raid may not have been as successful as the U.S. anticipated, but some consequences occurred from the strike. What was Japan's response to the raid?

Answer: The Japanese thought that the raid must have originated from the naval base on Midway Island. The maritime leadership decided that an attack on the island and its fleet would help prevent any further attacks and cripple the U.S. fleet even further. From the Doolittle Raid, the Battle of Midway came to fruition.

Two separate fleets attacked Midway. Who were the two Japanese admirals that led these fleets?

Answer: The main leader of the naval fleet was Admiral Isoroku Yamamoto, but the two admirals directly involved in the Battle of Midway were admirals Chūichi Nagumo and Nobutake Kondo.

The Allied forces landed in North Africa in 1942 and began the campaign dubbed Operation Torch. Where did the Allied forces land?

Answer: Two separate forces landed in North Africa: in Morocco and in Algeria.

In January of 1943, Roosevelt and Churchill met again. This time in Casablanca, Morocco. What was the purpose of the Casablanca Conference?

Answer: This was a meeting between the major leaders to discuss the strategic goals and plans for the remainder of the war. Stalin was invited but had to turn it down as he was dealing with the Stalingrad conflict.

There were several things discussed at the conference, but there were three main actions that were agreed upon. What were these actions?

Answer: Both leaders agreed that they should send aid to Russia to help them work on driving the German forces back. Another factor that was agreed upon was that the Allies needed to begin bombing key military locations within

Germany's borders. Lastly, the Battle of the Atlantic needed to be done with an Allied victory.

What was Operation Valkyrie?

Answer: This was one of many plots devised by dissidents within the German Government and military to assassinate Hitler.

Why did these individuals want Hitler dead?

Answer: Many of the elite political and military officials felt that Hitler was tarnishing the reputation of the entire country. They also felt that his ideologies and tactics were going to bring the Reich eventually to ruin.

After the assassination attempt, Hitler and his leadership began to conduct an in-depth investigation into the people involved. Some evidence suggested a very prominent general. This general, instead of being arrested, committed suicide. Who was this general?

Answer: One of the names that popped up on the list of potential conspirators was Erwin Rommel. Though there was no concrete evidence, Rommel knew that would not stop investigators from arresting and executing him. To take matters into his own hands, the decorated general hung himself.

Who was the German commander in Paris at the time of the Allied invasion of Northern France?

Answer: The commander of the German forces defending Paris when the Allied forces began the attack was Genera Dietrich von Choltitz.

Choltitz was a good soldier, but when the Allies began to attack Paris and it looked like it was over, what order did he defy?

Answer: Choltitz had been directly ordered to set explosives, and if the city looked like it was going to fall, he was to level the city and some of it is most ionic monuments. He couldn't bring himself to do it as he didn't want to be the one that would be blamed for destroying one of the most beautiful cities in Europe.

What was the code name for the Belarussian Offensive of Minsk?

Answer: The Belarusian Offensive that would take Minsk back was code-named Operation Bagration.

What was the mission objection of Operation Bagration?

Answer: There were two main objectives: to destroy the German Strategic Center and remove the German forces from Belarus. This, in turn, would be paramount to the liberation of the Belarusian state.

The Battle of the Philippine Sea was one of the quickest battles in the Pacific theater. What was it also known as?

Answer: The battle was a decidedly one-sided victory for the Allied forces as the 450 planes that were launched were quickly shot from the sky. That is why it became known as the "Marianas Turkey Shoot."

Who were the commanders involved in the Battle of the Philippine Sea?

Answer: On the U.S. side, the fleets were commanded by Admiral Raymond Spruance and Admiral Mitscher. For the Japanese, the fleet was led by Admiral Jisaburō Ozawa.

At the Yalta Conference, Stalin agreed to enter the Pacific Theater. What would the Russians gain from helping the Americans in the Pacific?

Answer: Roosevelt had agreed that the Russians would regain control of the lands lost to them in the Russo-Japanese War as well as the U.S. would recognize the independent nation of the Republic of Mongolia, which would become a Soviet satellite in the years after the war.

At the Yalta Conference, what was determined to be the fate of Germany after the war?

Answer: Germany and Berlin would be divided up into zones that would be controlled by the three Allies and the Soviet Union. Germany would be demilitarized and de-Nazified. They would also be responsible for all reparations.

Stalin also had some requests at the Yalta Conference. What were these?

Answer: Stalin demanded that the land that had been gained with the reinvasion of Poland in 1939 remain in the control of Russia. He also wanted the Polish Government that was in exile to be relieved of all their duties. The Russian leader did agree to allow other parties to participate in the Polish Government and that the elections held in Poland would be free and fair. He also wanted to ensure that the nations on the Russian border were friendly to the communist way of life.

What was one tactic the Germans used to obtain an advantage at the Battle of the Bulge?

Answer: The Germans had soldiers drop behind enemy lines and dress as American soldiers. They would disseminate false information and change road signs. Eventually, the American soldiers figured out that something was going on and began testing any suspicious soldiers with American trivia.

Why did the Battle of Iwo Jima take longer than expected?

Answer: The Japanese began using a new defense tactic. They built artillery posts using the camouflage of the natural landscape of the island. This idea was born in the mind of General Tadamichi Kuribayashi.

What are the two other challenges faced by U.S. forces on Iwo Jima?

Answer: The beaches of the island were the first hurdle as they were soft and ashy, making them hard to maneuver. The other issue was the Banzai attack of the forces that lay in wait.

The Battle of Berlin was the last major battle on the European front. What was the division of labor between the forces?

Answer: The Russians did most of the heavy lifting in this battle as they were in charge of the ground troops. The British and Americans provided support via the air.

The plan for the battle was to surround Berlin and then push in from all sides. When was the city finally surrounded?

Answer: Multiple Russian army divisions encircled Berlin on April 24th, 1945.

The last major battle of the Pacific was the battle of Okinawa. What code name was given to this operation?

Answer: The battle for Okinawa was given the code name Operation Iceberg.

Why was Okinawa so crucial for the Allies to take in its mission to defeat Japan?

Answer: Okinawa was a gateway onto the mainland of Japan. This meant that if the U.S. was able to capture it, the final invasion would be easier. On top of that, a critical

Japanese airbase was on the island, and by capturing it, the Allies would be able to keep Japanese aircraft from the skies, which would cripple any hope for the Japanese to deploy a significant defense.

When was Hitler actually declared dead?

Answer: Hitler's body and his wife's body were burned, which made the identification of the bodies difficult. It took quite a while for the declaration of death to become final. In 1956, Adolf Hitler was finally declared dead.

Where was Germany's unconditional surrender signed at?

Answer: The surrender was signed by a general from each nation, and it was signed at Reims. The generals that signed the document were: General Jodl for Germany, General Susloparov for Russia, General Sevez for France, and General Smith for the United States.

Historian

What time were the two bombs dropped on Hiroshima and Nagasaki?

Answer: The bomb that was dropped on Hiroshima was deployed at 8:15 in the morning, and the one on Nagasaki dropped at two minutes after eleven in the morning.

What date did Emperor Hirohito state that Japan would accept the declaration made at Potsdam?

Answer: Emperor Hirohito convened a council of ministers at midnight on August 9th. They discussed if it was possible to win the war after the destruction of the two cities by the United States' new weapon. It was determined that the war was lost, and on August 10th, word was sent to the U.S. forces that Japan would be surrendering.

In order to pull off the invasion of the beaches of Normandy, the Allied forces had to use some deceptive tactics. What were some of these?

Answer: Under the leadership of Eisenhower and Montgomery, the Allied command knew they had to keep a tight lip when it came to the preparation for this massive invasion. Knowing that Germans had spies in their midst as well as air surveillance, they were going to have to be especially sneaky. They created fake equipment and a fake army that was allegedly commanded by General George S. Patton. Allied intelligence also used radio communications that were filled with false information. They also captured and flipped German spies, sending them home to be their operatives and disseminate incorrect information and rumors.

Japan and Russia have been at odds for centuries, but when it comes to WWII, when did the two nations sign a peace treaty?

Answer: The two nations have never, to this very day, signed a peace treaty. In fact, they are still in discussion as the S. Kuril Islands remain a point of contention.

During the war, there was a chocolate shortage. What popular treat was invented to make up for it?

Answer: Though the world was in turmoil, there still needed to be some happiness. Unfortunately, the sweet delicacy that everyone relied on for a bit of a smile—chocolate—was limited during the war. An Italian pastry chef, Pietro Ferrero, used hazelnuts in his chocolate filing and called it Pasta Gianduja, which, in 1964, would get a name change and become the addictive sweet treat Nutella.

Hitler had a family that moved to England. In fact, his nephew served with the Allied troops. What was this nephew's name?

Answer: Born William Hitler, when the war broke out, he quickly changed his name to Willy Patrick Stuart-Houston. Willie was born in London and moved to the United States as a young boy. He served with the U.S. Navy during the war.

WWII was devastating, and the loss of life was massive. What country lost more lives than any other?

Answer: The loss of life was tragic and immense, but the country that bore the biggest brunt of this loss was Russia. Over the seven years of battle, they lost 27 million soldiers and civilians. After them, it would be China with 11 million, and Germany with seven million.

One of the most significant battles on the Eastern front of the European Theater was the Battle of Kursk. How many tanks were used at the Battle of Kursk?

Answer: This battle took thousands of soldiers and weapons. One of the most effective weapons used during this campaign was the tank. Approximately 6,000 tanks were used during the battle.

Germany found it challenging to cripple the British Air Force commands in its air space. What system helped keep the Germans from being able to do this?

Answer: The Dowding system, named after the RAF commander, kept the British Air Force alert and on guard. This system was a series of radio locations that combined radar ground defense with aircraft for a rapid defense response. This system was placed at crucial points along the English coast and kept the military commanders apprised of any German activity.

Who were the two critical figureheads of the German Workers' Party?

Answer: The leader of the party when Hitler became a member was Anton Drexler, and his right-hand was Dietrich Eckhart.

What were some of the laws passed when the Nuremberg Laws went into effect?

Answer: These laws were created to drive a wedge between the German Jews and the German people. German Jews were not allowed to fly the German flag, they could not serve in the military, and it was forbidden to fraternize with anyone of the Jewish community if you were a German citizen.

By the time the war officially broke out in 1939, how many concentration camps were there?

Answer: Six of these camps had finished basic construction by the time Hitler rolled into Poland. Dachau, Sachsenhausen, Buchenwald, Flossenbürg, Mauthausen, and Ravensbrück.

Among the six, there was one solely dedicated to women prisoners. What was the concentration camp's name?

Answer: The one with women was called Ravensbrück.

Where was the women's camp located?

Answer: Ravensbrück was built 50 miles north of Berlin.

Days before the Russians stumbled upon Auschwitz, the Germans got wind of the Russian Army's nearness. On January 17th, the SS officer ordered their men to do what?

Answer: Sensing that they would soon be discovered, the SS officers and command of the camp ordered that healthy prisoners be evacuated and sent to other camps deeper in

Germany. They had a choice between railroad cars or marching. This death march cost 15,000 people their lives.

What date did the Russian troops find the extermination camp, Birkenau?

Answer: The camp was discovered on January 27th, 1945.

The commander of Auschwitz was Rudolf Hoss. What happened to him after the camp had been liberated?

Answer: The SS commander was tried at both the Nuremberg trials as well as by the Polish Supreme National Tribunal. When tried in Poland, he was found guilty and hung in the camp near the main Gestapo building. This execution would be the last public one ever carried out in Poland.

The conditions of all the concentration camps had deteriorated quickly after prisoners from outlying camps had been evacuated into ones within German borders. Along with this deterioration came severe disease outbreaks. What disease led the Nazi leader of Bergen-Belsen to negotiate a truce with the Allied forces?

Answer: The camp was running rampant with Typhus and did not have the supplies to treat the problem. Knowing that it was either negotiate with the troops surrounding the camp or die, Commandant Josef Kramer began to discuss surrendering with the British commander.

Bergen-Belsen was found not through tactical intel but by being sighted from a military vehicle. Who were the first people to find the camp?

Answer: The camp was spotted by Lieutenant John Randall and his driver as they did some reconnaissance for the special air service.

At the closing months of the war, many of the concentration camps executed death marches, and this included Dachau. Where were the prisoners forced to march to?

Answer: The 7,000 prisoners deemed healthy enough were herded into lines and force-marched toward the city of Tegernsee.

Japan and Germany entered into an alliance that was aimed against the communist party. Why would Hitler sign an anti-communist treaty with the Japanese?

Answer: Both parties had Russia in mind when they signed the treaty. The Japanese had already dealt with Russia's expansionist ways in the Russo-Japanese War, and Hitler was sure that the same ideas would come into play once the war was actually underway. To stop this expansionism, the two Axis powers put their intentions down on paper.

What was the Stimulant Decree of 1940?

Answer: The Blitzkrieg was going to require the soldiers to fight long and hard. In 1940, Hitler and his military leadership decreed that 35 million tablets of Pervitin and Isophane be sent to the front line and distributed to the troops.

Why were Pervitin and Isophane used on the front lines?

Answer: Pervitin and Isophane were both forms of methamphetamines and were used to enhance the stamina of the soldiers. The use of this drug allowed them to stay up for days and march further without feeling fatigued.

After Norway fell to the Nazi invasion, they put in a government that was easy to control. Who was the leader of this puppet government?

Answer: The campaign was won thanks to a commander loyal to Vidkun Quisling. This was who was placed in power after the Germans took Norway. He was a pro-fascist who prescribed to the ideology of the Nazi Party.

Other than the command from the fascist-supporting commander, what was the final blow to the Norwegian resistance?

Answer: Seeing that their allies on the continent needed their assistance, the British reallocated troops from the Norwegian front to the French front. This troop withdrawal left the Norwegian forces depleted and unable to stand up against the more substantial opposition.

Blitzkrieg was the winning formula at the beginning of the war, but WWII was not the first test of this tactic. Where was this military maneuver first tested?

Answer: The Germans wanted to make sure that the idea of Blitzkrieg would work, so they sent troops to help the fascist dictator Franco in Spain during the Civil War in 1936.

Mussolini had taken power and pledged to deliver the glory of the Roman Empire back to Italy. This would mean he would have to conquer North Africa, so he began a campaign to do just that. But why did he not have German support when he launched this campaign?

Answer: When news of the campaign came to Hitler, he offered troops to Mussolini, but the dictator declined the offer. There were some hard feelings about the Battle of Britain and Hitler's decline of his help. Mussolini did not want to look inferior to Hitler, so he said it was a matter of national pride and politely declined his offer.

Other areas that Mussolini would have to expand into would be Greece and the Balkans. He would first start with Greece. However, the campaign did not go as planned. How long did it take Greek forces to push Italian troops back to Albania?

Answer: With a distinct advantage of knowing their landscape and being ready for the attack, the Greek forces pushed the Italian military back to Albania in just about a week.

Japan would take advantage of the fall of France to expand its territory into mainland Asia via Vietnam. Who was the leader of the French Colonial Government at the time?

Answer: The French had been in Vietnam for quite a while and established a colonial government that ran everything smoothly. The man in charge when the Japanese invaded was Jean Decoux.

In order for the Japanese to be successful in their invasion of Vietnam, they needed help from the inside. What were the two resistance groups that collaborated with the Japanese?

Answer: The two nationalist groups were Cao Dai and the Hòa Hảo.

When the Japanese took control of Vietnam, they could have placed their own government officials in control; instead, they opted to leave the colonial government in power. Why did the Japanese do this?

Answer: The Japanese knew that they could control the government with a small presence and did not have the resources to do anything more than that. They left the government in place and sent people to spy on them to make sure they were not doing anything to subvert Japanese control.

When Russia began its expansion into the Baltic nations, many of them simply had no way to fight back. However,

there was a resistance group in Estonia. What was the name of this group?

Answer: The unit that stood their ground against the encroaching Red Army was the Signal Battalion at Tallinn Station.

The expansionist agenda of the Russian Government into the Baltics was intended to grow the influence of communism. Before they could begin to shape the government in their image, they had to do a few things. What two things were done to ensure that the communist ideology was excepted?

Answer: In order to ensure they got their way in the governments of the Baltic states, Russian authorities would have to do a little political repression eliminating any candidates that were anti-communism, and then they would do mass deportation of 130,000 people that were also anti-communism.

There were eight tenets to the Atlantic Charter. What were they?

Answer: The eight tenets were territorial rights, freedom of self-determination, economic issues, disarmament, ethical goals, freedom of the seas, and a determination to work for a "world free of want and fear."

The U.S. declared war almost immediately, and since they had stayed out of the fray for the first few years, the Axis powers declared war on them. Once Roosevelt declared war, how long did it take the Axis powers to declare war back?

Answer: The U.S. declared war on December 8th officially, and three days later, both Japan and Germany declared war on the U.S. With that, the U.S. was formally part of the war effort.

The siege of Leningrad would last for such a long time that the people within the city had to get creative to find food. What were some of the ways that the people managed to survive the siege?

Answer: When you are hungry, you get creative, and the people of Leningrad had to do just that. Some would scrape off the paste used to apply wallpaper as it was made of potatoes. They would also boil leather and eat the jelly created from the process. Many would cook and eat weeds and plants. But eventually, they did resort to eating pets and the animals of the zoo before some turned to cannibalism.

The Wannsee Conference played a role in the Nuremberg trials. What was this role?

Answer: The minutes of the conference were meticulously taken, and they were entered in as evidence of the atrocities committed by the Nazi leadership.

The Doolittle Raid was retaliation for the attack on Pearl Harbor. How many planes were used in this raid?

Answer: The United States sent 16 B-25 bombers to strike strategic locations on the Japanese mainland.

During the Battle of Midway, the Japanese lost four aircraft carriers. What were their names?

Answer: The four aircraft carriers that were sunk by U.S. forces at the Battle of Midway were: the Akagi, Kaga, Sōryū, and the Hiryū.

The Battle of Midway was a devastating naval loss for the Japanese. How many lives and ships were lost during the battle?

Answer: The Japanese lost 3,000 men, 300 aircraft, four aircraft carriers, and one heavy cruiser.

The U.S. losses at Midway were not as extensive but still massive. What were the losses experienced at the battle?

Answer: The U.S. lost 360 men, 145 planes, and two ships—the Yorktown and Hammann.

What was the British 7th Armored Division nicknamed?

Answer: The division that led the Tunisian campaign was called the "Desert Rats."

Erwin Rommel was the commander of the German forces in North Africa. What divisions did he have control over?

Answer: Rommel was a respected general and led the 5th Light Division as well as the 15th Panzer Division to many successes before being defeated by the Allied push into North Africa known as Operation Torch.

Rommel had many victories, but one of his first and most significant was where?

Answer: The Battle for Benghazi came to an end in April 1941. This was a resounding victory for the general and spurred him on to even more conflicts across Northern Africa.

Stalingrad was another siege-like situation, and Stalin didn't want a repeat of Leningrad. But he also didn't want to give way to the Germans, so he sent down Order No. 227. What was this order?

Answer: This was an order that instructed his forces at Stalingrad not to give an inch. Those that surrendered would face a trial and potential execution.

Who was the German general who surrendered at the Battle of Stalingrad?

Answer: The general who had to admit defeat was General Friedrich von Paulus.

To break the Germans' hold on Stalingrad, the Russian military leaders crafted Operation Uranus. Who were the generals in charge of its execution?

Answer: This Russian counteroffensive stationed armies in the hills surrounding Stalingrad was led by Generals Georgy Zhukov, Aleksandr Vasilevsky, and Nikolay Voronov.

To keep the conference secret, there needed to be a code name for the meeting. What was the one chosen for the Casablanca Conference?

Answer: The code name used in all communications was SYMBOL.

What was the Kursk Salient?

Answer: The Kursk Salient was a bulge in the nettle lines around the land near Kursk. The bulge created a breach line 250 miles south and north of Kursk as well as 100 miles east and west of the city. Kursk was an important location because of its access to railways and roads for supplies transportation.

For Operation Citadel to be successful, Hitler needed to replenish his troops after the Battle of Stalingrad. How did he replenish his troop levels?

Answer: Hitler became desperate and began drafting military veterans up to the age of 50. He also changed the rule concerning youth and enlisted them as well.

Operation Citadel was a counteroffensive aimed at taking Kursk using the salient as a means of entry. When was the operation due to be executed?

Answer: The official launch day of the campaign was set for May 3rd, 1943. However, the operation was delayed.

Why did Hitler delay Operation Citadel?

Answer: Hitler, despite his commander's suggestion, delayed the operation for better weather to allow time for his new Panther and Tiger tanks to be delivered to the front line.

After the delay of Operation Citadel, when did it get started?

Answer: The actual execution of Operation Citadel took place on July 5th, 1945.

Operation Citadel opened up the way for the Battle of Kursk. This was a bloody battle that left both sides with large casualty counts. How many soldiers were lost on each side?

Answer: The Soviet Army lost 800,000 men, and the Germans lost 200,000 men.

Who were the main men involved in Operation Valkyrie?

Answer: The actual assailant was Claus von Stauffenberg, the chief of staff of the German reserves, along with Stauffenberg, as well as Berlin police chief Arthur Nebe, Eduard Wagner, Henning von Tresckow, and many others.

What was the opening maneuver in Operation Bagration?

Answer: The operation started with Belarusian Guerilla fighters setting and igniting explosives around the railway hubs used for transportation.

How many planes on each side were lost in the Battle of the Philippine Sea?

Answer: The Japanese, over the two separate attacks, lost approximately 480 aircraft, while the U.S. fleet lost 29.

After Russian troops began to move into Berlin, what was the first interior ministry building they took charge of?

Answer: The Russian troops moved into Berlin with the mission of taking major tactical points throughout the city. This included significant government buildings, and the first one that they were able to take was the Gestapo headquarters.

Who was the Japanese general that led the forces on Okinawa?

Answer: Lieutenant General Mitsuru Ushijima commanded 130,000 men as well as a small contingent of Boritai. These were local civilians that had been conscripted into service.

What happened to General Susloparov after the signing of Germany's surrender at Reims?

Answer: Stalin was furious as he had not been permitted to sign the surrender. He was ordered back to the capital and found himself in the hands of the secret police.

Acknowledgments

This is a special thanks to the following history lovers who have taken time out of their busy schedule to be part of the History Compacted Launch Team. Thank you all so much for all the feedback and support. Let's continue our journey to simplify the stories of history!

Steve Thomson, Bill Anderson, Karol Pietka, Patricia King, Janel Iverson, Dave Kaiser, Christian Loucq, Dwight Waller, Anthony Rodriguez, Ricky Burk, Rick Conley, Holli-Marie Taylor, Ray Workman, Judy Kirkbride, Kim Lyon, Simon Hardy, Casey Bates, Matthew Peters, Kevin Gilhooly, Charles Hallett

About History Compacted

Here in History Compacted, we see history as a large collection of stories. Each of these amazing stories of the past can help spark ideas for the future. However, history is often proceeded as boring and incomprehensible. That is why it is our mission to simplify the fascinating stories of history.

Visit Us At: www.historycompacted.com

Dark Minds In History

For updates about new releases, as well as exclusive promotions, sign up for our newsletter and you can also receive a free book today. Thank you and see you soon.

Sign up here: http://bit.ly/2ToHti3

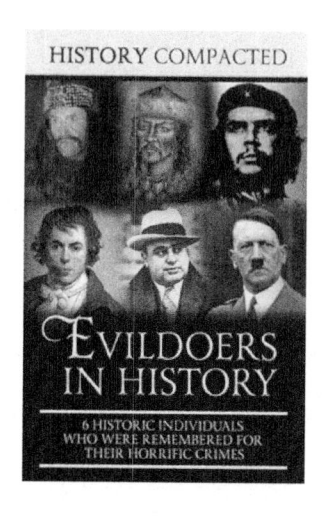

Evildoers in History: 6 Historic Individuals Remembered For Their Horrific Crimes is a book that explores the stories of six infamous criminals in history, these evildoers were not remembered by their countless murders but by the brutality with which they took the lives of their victims. There is no other term to describe them but ruthless, as you will soon find out.

Prepare yourself, the gruesome part of history is not for everyone...

Printed in Great Britain
by Amazon